‖‖‖ ‖ ‖‖‖‖‖‖ ‖‖ ‖ ‖ ‖‖‖ ‖‖‖‖‖‖‖‖ ‖ ‖‖

📖 **W9-BDE-172**

Praise for
Disruptive Classroom Technologies
by Sonny Magana

Sonny Magana has made a significant contribution to innovation in education with his important book, *Disruptive Classroom Technologies*, and the T3 Framework. There have been 161 meta-analyses on various aspects of computers in education—from 10,226 studies, and the average effect is $d = 0.34$—and this effect has not changed over the past 50 years despite phenomenal changes in the technology. A major reason for this lack of impact is that most technological interventions do not change the dominant "tell and practice" teaching model. Moving beyond translation and transforming current practice to transcendent uses of technology is clearly where we should go. We need to build collaborative communities of students solving problems, explaining to others (regardless of ability), and using the social media aspects of technology to change classroom conversations from monologue to dialogue, increasing student impact questions and allowing errors to be stated and dealt with— this can be so transcendental. This is the core of Magana's claims, and indeed, this is how we'll see technology really make the difference we're after!

—**John Hattie**, Laureate Professor, Deputy Dean of MGSE
Director of the Melbourne Education Research Institute
Melbourne Graduate School of Education
University of Melbourne, Australia
Chair, Board of the Australian Institute for Teaching and School Leadership
Associate Director of the ARC-SRI: Science of Learning Research

The T3 Framework is a brilliant breakthrough in our understanding and use of technology for learning. Sonny Magana clearly portrays the nature and difference between translational, transformational, and transcendent use of technology. The identification of transcendent use is itself an innovation. On top of all this he shows us how to navigate through the T3 system with guiding questions, prompts, and rubrics. For those of us working on the frontier of deep learning, *Disruptive Classroom Technologies* and the T3 Framework are much-needed gifts.

—**Michael Fullan,** Professor Emeritus
OISE/University of Toronto
Toronto, Canada

Fresh, innovative, and revolutionary, Sonny Magana's T3 Framework promises to challenge the status quo and invite disruptive practices in educational technology. Enhancing social entrepreneurship with technology, the final stage of Magana's framework for technology use in education, is a powerful proposal and a compelling vision worth pursuing by all educators.

—**Yong Zhao**, PhD
Foundation Distinguished Professor, University of Kansas
Co-Author, *Never Send a Human to Do a Machine's Job: Correcting Top 5 Ed Tech Mistakes*
Lawrence, KS

Sonny Magana's T3 Framework will provide schools and districts with the planning tools needed to go beyond the "$1,000 pencil." His concept of technology as a disruptive force is exactly how we should be thinking about this historic moment of redesigning the culture of learning. Magana's book is filled with powerful stories and thoughtful questions that will inspire and empower educators to improve learning. Moreover, he has provided us with a framework for implementation with detail that simply has not existed with earlier models. I have known Sonny Magana for twenty years. His wisdom comes from his incredible passion as an educator, school administrator, and now, as a researcher.

—**Alan November**, Founder, November Learning
Author, *Empowering Students With Technology*

Sonny Magana carefully analyzes innovation in education and adoption of technology through his T3 lens, providing practical tools and examples to assist us all. He draws on colorful, helpful examples, from music to the fall of the iron curtain, to illustrate his ideas and highlight pathways from translational through transformational and, ultimately, to transcendent technology use. *Disruptive Classroom Technologies* exemplifies an "innovate, don't digitize" message and should encourage us all to progress quickly beyond the nursery slopes of adoption to the highly productive and exciting upper reaches of technology use for education.

—**Gavin Dykes,** Program Director
Education World Forum
London, United Kingdom

What if . . . what if there were a framework to make tangible in a very articulate, strategic, and actionable way what we have long sought to implement: the student use of technologies to inspire learning that matters? Dr. Magana has done it! *Disruptive Classroom Technologies* validates your experience and then effortlessly and exponentially moves you along the T3 continuum to transcendent impact from the use of educational technology. A must-read for educational leaders at all levels. Magana helps us add value to our investment in technology, and create educational systems of limitless learning.

—**Dr. Mary Wegner,** Superintendent
Sitka School District
Sitka, AK

Disruptive Classroom Technologies is a model for how to effectively implement technology in a school. Dr. Magana's writing and practice demonstrate his unique combination of having a deep understanding of effective pedagogical practice and cutting-edge knowledge about technology. The T3 Framework that Dr. Magana developed blends learning and technology together in an applicable and effective manner. I have personally observed the power of Dr. Magana's work in our own school district; Gaylord Community Schools has embraced the T3 Framework, and, as a result, is a better place for students to learn and staff to teach.

—**Brian Pearson,** Superintendent
Gaylord Community Schools
Gaylord, MI

In *Disruptive Classroom Technologies*, Sonny Magana brilliantly defines the T3 Framework, which serves as a "call to action" for all education leaders to examine the role that technology has in teaching and learning. As Magana details, schools are technology rich and innovation poor due to a constant pursuit of the latest glitzy technology fad that often has limited additive value to student achievement. As education leaders, we must see beyond the frenzy of the latest technology craze and evaluate the value-added impact that technology resources have on teaching and learning. The T3 Framework provides a structure for educators to evaluate technology resources and to make education decisions that ensure we are transforming and transcending our classrooms. *Disruptive Classroom Technologies* is a must-read for all educators!

—**Rick Oser,** Principal
Lemon Grove Academy
Lemon Grove, CA

In *Disruptive Classroom Technologies*, Dr. Sonny Magana introduces the T3 Framework, a tool simple enough for our students and staff to understand and begin to use immediately. Our staff and students found the T3 Framework easy to grasp; yet, once fully implemented, it will effectively transform the discussion on technology integration and how to significantly utilize education's investment in technology to enhance teaching and learning. In an authentic and meaningful way, the use of T3 will not only allow our students and teachers to focus on the content of today, but to develop the relevant skills and mindsets needed for the world of tomorrow.

—**Gregory A. Rayl,** MEd, Superintendent
American International School of Lagos
Lagos, Nigeria

A must-read for educational leaders faced with a "technology rich but innovative poor" school, *Disruptive Classroom Technologies* reframes how educators and students use digital tools in the pursuit of transcendent learning. Equipped with the easy-to-understand T3 Framework, teachers can quickly assess where their own and their students' use of technology resides: at the translational, transformational, and transcendent level. Including advice and real-world examples of how to move students' use of digital tools from simple consumption to social entrepreneurship, *Disruptive Classroom Technologies* equips teachers and leaders with the tools and mindset necessary to engage students as active architects of their learning in a solution-driven, global community of learners.

—**Kim Rayl,** MEd, Curriculum Director
American International School of Lagos
Lagos, Nigeria

Change isn't coming . . . it's already on our doorstep. The disruptive nature of technology compels all educators to critically evaluate integration in support of improved learning outcomes. The T3 Framework developed by Sonny Magana provides a much-needed tool for all educators to harness the positive aspects of disruptive technologies to support learning.

—**Eric Sheninger,** Author and Senior Fellow
International Center for Leadership in Education

A terrific book! Anyone who can draw upon the Beatles, the Soviet Union, and Eddie Van Halen to illustrate technology in education, as Dr. Sonny Magana does in *Disruptive Classroom Technologies*, clearly has it going on!

- Leaders: Keep this book by your side for inspiration, insight, and ideas for leading innovative classroom practice.
- Teachers: The T3 Framework will focus your daily teaching practices and hone your natural instincts for innovative instruction and learning with technology.
- Teachers and Leaders: Take the T3 challenge! Can you empower your students to the transcendent level of content understanding using disruptive technologies?

—**Tom Charouhas,** Digital Media Teacher
Rose Hill Middle School
Redmond, WA

This is the book that can disrupt the future trajectory of education. *Disruptive Classroom Technologies* is the book that could help education evolve into a proper digital-age system that will empower students to be in control of their own future, no matter what that may hold.

—**Dr. L. Robert Furman,** Principal
South Park Elementary School
South Park, PA

Dr. Magana gets to the heart of how to create transcendent learning environments, clearly demonstrating the role technology can play in driving social entrepreneurship and change. This book is different than most: Dr. Magana has artfully captured the importance of technology in the larger context of transcending traditional learning, using technology to better engage learners, solve difficult problems, and improve results.

—**Renee Patton,** Director of Education
Cisco Public Sector
Stanford, CA

Developing students who are active, informed, and capable of taking action in the real world is at the heart of *Disruptive Classroom Technologies*. Sonny Magana has shared a new research- and evidence-based framework to guide our thinking about innovation in education, aptly identifying students' "passion and purpose" as the key drivers for school improvement. This book should challenge leaders and teachers alike to review expectations around how and why they lever digital tools in contemporary learning design.

—**Mark Sparvell,** Senior Education Manager
School Leader Audience Strategy
Worldwide Education Team, Microsoft
Redmond, WA

If there is one book all educational leaders read, make it this one. Creating learning environments that promote and foster innovation in both teaching and learning are essential today. Education is ripe for disruption, and Sonny Magana has provided a clear framework for helping students and teachers to do more. The T3 Framework can provide guidance to all educational leaders and create the learning students need and deserve.

—**Steven W. Anderson,** Digital Learning and Relationship Evangelist
West Corporation
Winston-Salem, NC

Disruptive Classroom Technologies provides concrete and clearly defined descriptors for each level of the T3 Framework. Compared with existing frameworks, the T3 Framework makes it easier to classify observed classroom examples of technology integration—and I predict it will be more intuitive for teachers to visualize moving to the higher levels of the T3 Framework. As a district that's working with the New Pedagogies for Deep Learning hub, I really value the alignment of T2 and T3 with deep learning progressions, particularly leveraging digital tools for developing creative ideas and supporting effective leadership for action.

—**Bill Palmer,** Director of Teaching and Learning
and Technology Integration
Bellingham Public Schools
Bellingham, WA

Technology is a very real and prevalent part of today's society, and as educators who are preparing students to become successful in this society, it is essential that we use it to enhance student learning in an effective and meaningful way. *Disruptive Classroom Technologies* provides a framework for how to obtain that technological knowledge.

—**Allison Greene,** Third-Grade Teacher
Hoffman Elementary School
Glenview, IL

This excellent book gives school leaders authoritative guidance about what the future could look like in their schools. This book is essential reading for school leaders at every level. What I like about this book is that it gives a structure for personal and vicarious learning about the real matter of school leadership so that these accumulated experiences and wisdom are not lost at either the personal or collegial levels.

—**Dr. Neil MacNeill,** Head Master
Ellenbrook Independent Primary School
Ellenbrook, Australia

As districts struggle to truly embed technology into the daily classroom learning, it is becoming clear that a new set of language and ideas is needed to move this work forward. This book provides readers with a fresh framework that can build institutional capacity and deeper integration of education technology.

—**Dr. Robert Dillon,** Director
BrightBytes Institute
San Francisco, CA

Educators are struggling to navigate classroom environments that are increasingly disrupted by new and emerging technology. In *Disruptive Classroom Technologies*, Magana helps to make the ambiguity of the current landscape something to both look forward to and to harness. There is no better or more important time to be a teacher, and any self-reflecting leader or educator will benefit from the intentionality of Magana's T3 Framework.

—**Erin Bown-Anderson,** Director of Technology Integration
Austin Independent School District
Austin, TX

Disruptive Classroom Technologies offers a timely and practical approach to taming the disjointed adoption of technology in schools today. A trademark of Dr. Magana's work is its ability to be applied immediately in schools to shift the paradigm of classroom innovation. This text gives the practitioner an actionable level of understanding through a realistic framework.

—**Darin Knicely,** EdS, Ed Tech Entrepreneur and School Leader
Old Dominion University
Alexandria, VA

In *Disruptive Classroom Technologies*, Sonny Magana captures precisely the transformational nature of the iEARN global network's peer-to-peer interaction and authentic learning, pointing out that this transformation takes place in educators as well as in students as both learn with the world instead of just about it. Dr. Magana accurately, and to my knowledge, uniquely, describes this classroom approach as a start-up entrepreneurial endeavor where the teacher becomes the "learning manager" in a setting in which students make meaningful contributions through problem solving and inquisitive interaction. With the depth and breadth of varied experiences both in and outside the classroom, Dr. Magana is able to peel apart the many layers of effective teaching and learning and identify a coherent T3 Framework.

—**Dr. Edwin H. Gragert,** PhD, Executive Director Emeritus
iEARN-USA
New York, NY

The T3 Framework provides a measurable, hierarchical model for guiding technology usage in the classroom. It provides educators with a way to inspect their current practices and establish a clear path to purposeful technology use in order to engage their students. The true power of T3 is the operationalizing of theory for direct application to the classroom setting. *Disruptive Classroom Technologies* will resonate with any educator who wants to maximize the impact of technology on instruction.

—**James Corns,** Director Digital Safety and Innovation
Baltimore County Public Schools
Baltimore, MD

With the plethora of technology tools to choose from, busy teachers and administrators are at a loss when deciding which tools will help improve learning. Sonny Magana's T3 Framework is a timely solution to this problem. The self-evaluative matrices, questionnaires, and framing tools make the task of transforming one's teaching achievable. *Disruptive Classroom Technologies* will take a place of honor on my bookshelf, right next to Friedman and Bonk!

—**Jan Zanetis,** Managing Director
Center for Interactive Learning and Collaboration
Nashville, TN

As schools and other institutions of learning struggle to keep pace with the evolving demands and challenges of educating, "today's learners for tomorrow's future" questions persist about the investment and value technology brings to the work of teaching and learning. Anchored in authoritative research on known, high-yield pedagogical practice, and building on the prevailing TPACK and SAMR frameworks, Magana presents a refined and structured approach to thinking about technology in instruction that minimizes ambiguity, misinterpretation, and the low-level application of educational technology in schools. The T3 Framework provides an actionable and forward-thinking model that explicitly addresses these value-added objectives while adding a new dimension for leading learners to a place of transcendent technology use, where inquiry design and social entrepreneurship seek to address pressing concerns of social justice and the application of technology to solve complex problems that are personal, communal, and global in nature. This is a must-read book for anyone who wants to ensure that technology in schools is used as a force multiplier to truly power student learning, agency, and the development of skills to thrive as contributing architects of this century's knowledge economy.

—**Carl Fahle,** Information Technology Director
Educational Technology Leader
South San Francisco, Unified School District
San Francisco, CA

Sustainable innovation in education is not about designing something new and flashy. Authentic innovation that positively transforms student learning and success only comes from the development of relationships among students and teachers. Dr. Magana's work is vital because it is a call to design learning environments that support teachers while also engaging students in challenging curriculum and activities. Transformation only occurs when school systems focus on enhancing the roles, interactions, and expectations of what our students and educators can accomplish. By increasing authentic learning partnerships, educators increase the potential to tap into students' passions to solve issues, challenges, and problems that exist today. Dr. Magana's new T3 Framework helps guide this work to ignite the commitments of educators and students through the effective integration of technology into teaching and learning.

—**Ivan Duran,** EdD, Assistant Superintendent
Dallas Independent School District
Dallas, TX

Emerging economies are making huge investments in information communication technology (ICT) aimed at improving student learning outcomes. However, these investments are not paying off, for lack of a coherent road map that leads to substantive student learning. Sonny Magana's T3 Framework is the much-needed innovation that can change this situation. His framework will be easily understood by policy makers, and furthermore, it allows for development planners to efficiently prepare program costing, design implementation arrangements, and prepare an effective monitoring mechanism for maximum impact of ICT in education. Let's raise the T3 flag and transform education for all!

—**John W. Henly,** International Education Adviser
Dhaka, Bangladesh

Today's learning environments necessitate the use of technology, and now they have been given a big boost by Dr. Magana's contribution of the T3 Framework. Magana introduces a common vocabulary clearly organized and accessible within a taxonomy of stages. The T3s are not just for K–12 classrooms; rather, coaches, consultants, and trainers designing online professional development courses will find nuggets of knowledge within the Framework. One will "strike gold" when learners are moved toward positive, inclusive, and communal responses.

—**Gretchen Dobson**, EdD, Global Strategist
Academic Assembly, Inc.
Brisbane, Australia

As a leader and innovator in technology integration, Dr. Magana supportively challenges educators to disrupt conventional ways of conceptualizing and engaging technology in classroom settings. The T3 Framework provides a practical and user-friendly model for pushing beyond the traditional boundaries that tend to limit effective technology applications in education. Technology integration in teaching and learning holds great promise for enhancing student engagement and achievement in useful and wonderful ways. The T3 Framework shows us how.

—**Laurie Stevahn**, Professor of Educational Leadership
College of Education, Seattle University
Seattle, WA

This is a must-read for any change maker truly invested in making a difference with the use of technology in the classroom. Dr. Magana's T3 Framework provides the in-depth guidance needed for any learning organization embracing a "disruptive" approach to technology use. The methodology to achieve transcendence with both teachers and students alike is fascinating. Readers will embrace the theory backed by action.

—**Jose Reyes**, EdD, Director of Adult and Alternative School
Central Unified School District
Fresno, CA

Understanding Sonny Magana's background and past work, I had high expectations, but *Disruptive Classroom Technologies* was even better than I had expected. I so enjoyed this work and got so much from it that I can't wait to start sharing it with schools immediately. Magana outlines the truly personal and relevant use of technology by students—to understand, hypothesize, innovate, and solve the "wicked real-life problems that matter to *them*." The T3 Framework will require some serious reflective, honest, and thoughtful effort from district leaders and faculty, but the potential student rewards and outcomes cannot be maximized without this key piece. I believe the real power of *Disruptive Classroom Technologies* and the T3 Framework lies in the guided step-by-step approach Magana has developed for setting vision and goal setting, and to building consensus, belief, and mastery in their plans. This is an absolutely *great* work!

—**Mike Belcher**, Director of EdTech Innovation
HP, Inc.
Austin, TX

For Tracey: I can't do
anything except be in love with you.

Disruptive Classroom Technologies

A Framework for Innovation in Education

Sonny Magana

Foreword by Robert J. Marzano

CORWIN
A SAGE Publishing Company

FOR INFORMATION:

Corwin

A SAGE Company

2455 Teller Road

Thousand Oaks, California 91320

(800) 233-9936

www.corwin.com

SAGE Publications Ltd.

1 Oliver's Yard

55 City Road

London EC1Y 1SP

United Kingdom

SAGE Publications India Pvt. Ltd.

B 1/I 1 Mohan Cooperative Industrial Area

Mathura Road, New Delhi 110 044

India

SAGE Publications Asia-Pacific Pte. Ltd.

3 Church Street

#10-04 Samsung Hub

Singapore 049483

Acquisitions Editor: Ariel Bartlett

Senior Associate Editor: Desirée A. Bartlett

Editorial Assistant: Kaitlyn Irwin

Production Editor: Melanie Birdsall

Copy Editor: Meg Granger

Typesetter: C&M Digitals (P) Ltd.

Proofreader: Annie Lubinsky

Indexer: Molly Hall

Cover Designer: Janet Kiesel

Marketing Manager: Anna Mesick

Copyright © 2017 by Corwin

All rights reserved. When forms and sample documents are included, their use is authorized only by educators, local school sites, and/or noncommercial or nonprofit entities that have purchased the book. Except for that usage, no part of this book may be reproduced or utilized in any form or by any means, electronic or mechanical, including photocopying, recording, or by any information storage and retrieval system, without permission in writing from the publisher.

All trademarks depicted within this book, including trademarks appearing as part of a screenshot, figure, or other image, are included solely for the purpose of illustration and are the property of their respective holders. The use of the trademarks in no way indicates any relationship with, or endorsement by, the holders of said trademarks.

Printed in the United States of America

ISBN 978-1-5063-5909-0

This book is printed on acid-free paper.

17 18 19 20 21 10 9 8 7 6 5 4 3 2 1

DISCLAIMER: This book may direct you to access third-party content via web links, QR codes, or other scannable technologies, which are provided for your reference by the author(s). Corwin makes no guarantee that such third-party content will be available for your use and encourages you to review the terms and conditions of such third-party content. Corwin takes no responsibility and assumes no liability for your use of any third-party content, nor does Corwin approve, sponsor, endorse, verify, or certify such third-party content.

CONTENTS

PART II • STAGES OF THE T3 FRAMEWORK

PART III • PUTTING THE T3 FRAMEWORK TO USE

Download resources at
www.corwin.com/disruptiveclassroomtech
under the "Preview" tab.

FIGURES AND TABLES

FIGURES

TABLES

FOREWORD

I have had the good fortune to know and work with Dr. Sonny Magana for over ten years. During that time, I have grown to trust him as a friend and confidant. Equally important, I have grown to view him as a visionary leader regarding what K–12 education can be if we truly embrace the potential of technology. Additionally, I have grown to perceive him as a person who helps me keep my gaze on the horizon as opposed to the terrain immediately in front of me. This book should do the same for readers relative to the last two perceptions.

The central thesis of *Disruptive Classroom Technologies* is that the uses of technologies can be organized into three hierarchically ordered domains in what Magana calls the T3 Framework: translational, transformational, and transcendent. Translational uses of technology help educators perform tasks in which they are currently engaged. Using technology in this way saves time, provides more accuracy, and makes the execution of tasks more efficient. Tasks which are commonly addressed from a translational perspective include data storage and record keeping, reporting, communicating, testing, grading, and budgeting, to name a few. Many districts and schools limit their use of technology to the translational level. This level is certainly important, and Magana advises that it should be systematically addressed, well monitored, and continually updated. However, stopping at this level is a mistake all too often made.

Transformational uses of technology don't simply aid in the execution of current tasks. Rather, they redefine old tasks and generate new opportunities. Of the various examples of transformational use of technology that Magana provides, the one on which he spends the majority of time is the design and use of mastery goals. Simply stated, a mastery orientation is one that (1) provides students with timely and accurate feedback regarding their current status and growth on specific topics, (2) provides students with clear guidance as to how they might improve and the instructional resources to do so, and (3) provides students with multiple opportunities to demonstrate proficiency and monitors their progress within and between topics. These three functions when attempted without the aid of technology are almost impossible to do. However, at this level so much of the workload can and should be absorbed by technology, and the primary role of the teacher shifts to guidance and support as opposed to providing information.

Transcendent uses of technology represent the top level of Magana's system. The starting point for this level of use is student passion, and the ending point involves moving students from focusing solely on their own concerns to concerns about the greater good of their local and extended communities. Such a focus has the power to shift one's consciousness outside current circumstances. Indeed, this is at the heart of the meaning of transcendence—shifting one's perspective from idiosyncratic and myopic to communal and all inclusive. At this level, technology has an instrumental function. It cannot provide transcendent experiences, but it can help students create experiences that are transcendental to them with the guidance and support of the teacher. In effect, the teacher becomes as important to this process as the technology. It is at this level that the entire system changes.

In one way, the T3 Framework can be thought of as utilitarian in that it provides a way to think about the uses of technology that is immediately useful. In another way, Magana's framework can be thought of as highly disruptive because it demonstrates how much work remains if we are to deliver on the bright promise of technology that many educators saw and articulated decades ago. Unfortunately, that bright promise is still in the distance, somewhere on the horizon. If one views schools and schooling through the lens of Magana's framework, though, that horizon can become clearer, more attainable, and more inspirational.

—**Robert J. Marzano**
Chief Academic Officer
Marzano Research

ACKNOWLEDGMENTS

I am deeply honored to have had the good fortune of learning from and working with my lifelong friend and mentor, Dr. Robert J. Marzano. Without his caring support and inspiration, this book would not have come to fruition. I would like to express my deepest gratitude and admiration to Professors John J. Gardiner and Laurie Stevahn from Seattle University; Rick Oser, Carla Taugher-Aranda, Jessica Casillas, and the wonderful educators and students at Lemon Grove Academy in Lemon Grove, California; Brian Pearson and the outstanding educators of Gaylord Community Schools in Gaylord, Michigan; and Greg Rayl, Kim Rayl, Jim Larrison, Chukwudi Asobo, Bola Body-Lawson, Sara Bakulski, and the amazing educators and students at the American International School in Lagos, Nigeria. I hope you find this book to be worthy of the transcendent work you do on a daily basis.

PUBLISHER'S ACKNOWLEDGMENTS

Corwin gratefully acknowledges the contributions of the following reviewers:

Dr. Robert Dillon, Director
BrightBytes Institute
San Francisco, CA

Dr. Neil MacNeill, Head Master
Ellenbrook Independent Primary School
Ellenbrook, Australia

ABOUT THE AUTHOR

 **Dr. Anthony J. "Sonny" Magana III, EdD,** is an award-winning educator, best-selling author, and pioneering educational technology researcher. Sonny is a highly sought-after leadership consultant and instructional coach with more than 30 years' experience transforming learning systems around the world. Sonny is the author of numerous research studies and articles, and his first book, *Enhancing the Art and Science of Teaching With Technology*, coauthored with Dr. Robert J. Marzano, achieved international acclaim.

A tireless advocate for transcending the status quo, Sonny founded and served as principal of Washington State's first CyberSchool in 1996, a groundbreaking blended learning program that continues to meet the needs of at-risk students in Washington. He is a recipient of the prestigious Milken Family Foundation National Educator Award and the Governor's Commendation for Educational Excellence. An avid musician, yoga practitioner, and beekeeper, Sonny holds a bachelor of science degree from Stockton University, a master of education degree from City University (where he was honored with the Presidential Award for meritorious scholarship), an educational administration endorsement, and a doctorate in educational leadership from Seattle University.

PREFACE

WHO SHOULD READ THIS BOOK?

It is my sincere hope that anyone with an interest in and passion for modernizing educational systems with digital tools will find this book to be a valuable investment of their time. This work is the result of a 30-year investment in resolving a wicked problem that matters to me: How can learning systems reliably harness the potential of digital tools to accelerate instructional quality and student learning productivity? It's a wicked problem because there are, and will continue to be, too many variables to consider, too many digital tools to juggle, and too much evidence-free propaganda confounding our thinking about technology in education.

The implication of this problem is that we seem to have an overabundance of low-value technology use and little high- or very-high-value technology use in our classrooms. Have we developed, at considerable cost and energy, learning environments that are digitally rich and innovation poor? I've been trying to make some sense of it all for the better part of my adult life. I devised the T3 Framework as an evidence-based signal amid all the noise bombarding teachers, school and district leaders, instructional coaches, school board members, policy makers, and educational futurists who are passionate about using digital tools to unleash students' limitless learning potential; in the end, this book is for those who believe, as I do, that the purpose of education is to prepare students for *their* future, not their education system's past.

WHERE ARE WE AND WHERE ARE WE GOING?

Lately, much has been said and written about the need to prepare today's learners for the forthcoming knowledge society: a society in which conceptual understanding and the generation of new ideas and narratives reign supreme. But humans have always lived in knowledge societies. As sentient beings, we have adapted and advanced, over time becoming apex learning machines whose capacity for creativity, critical thinking, and contributive knowledge generation has enabled our species to survive and thrive in unforgivingly harsh environments. In addition to our giant brains and remarkably sophisticated means of self-expression, part of what makes humans stand far apart is our extraordinary capacity for developing and applying disruptive technologies not only to make life easier and better in the moment but to archive our knowledge base for future generations. From the earliest cave drawings to the Dead Sea Scrolls to wikis and blogs, the natural human impulse to leave behind something of value for future generations to have long after we expire may very well be unique to our species.

Human knowledge development and expression has experienced two greatly disruptive periods. The first was marked by the invention of the Gutenberg printing press, a machine that caused disruptions by enabling an unprecedented explosion in human knowledge and the forms in which that knowledge was represented, through the mass-produced written word. Another great period of disruption was marked by man's ability to harness various forms of combustive and excited-electron energy to power new machinery for industry, engineering, production, transportation, entertainment, and lighting for nocturnal activities.

Schwarz (2010) suggests that we are currently in the infancy of a third great period of disruption—one that is marked by the rise of digital technologies powered by the syntax of the binary code. Digital technologies enable entirely new ways of representing human knowledge that are easily archivable and as readily accessible to toddlers as they are to centenarians. This new digital era will see the exponential growth of a globally connected, interdependent network of knowledge architects actively designing, producing, and contributing new digital representations of human knowledge and thought.

> Digital technologies enable entirely new ways of representing human knowledge that are easily archivable and as readily accessible to toddlers as they are to centenarians.

Why then, in this period of digital disruption, do school systems, particularly those serving our neediest and most disenfranchised learners, use analog tools and worksheets as the primary way to make student thinking and knowledge gain apparent to teachers, parents, and education stakeholders? While some of these learning environments incorporate the use of technology tools, the ways these digital tools are used have generally added little value. Why haven't the environments that serve our youth, our most precious natural resource, been significantly transformed by the application of disruptive technologies?

This is a highly complex problem with many contributing variables. However, an essential question appears to be missing in the current narrative of educational technology: How does the use of technology add value, in terms of unleashing student learning potential, in ways that are not possible without the technology? Indeed, some of you may be asking, quite rightly, does technology add any value at all? Educational systems would benefit from a clearly structured and incremental approach to adding value through technology integration that will help educators and leaders (1) address the current use of classroom technologies, (2) establish clear goals for continuous growth and mastery, and (3) measure and track progress toward those goals. Adopting such an approach would help schools realize the untapped potential of educational technologies to serve modern learners who thrive when given multiple options for creatively representing their knowledge gain and thinking pathways with modern tools.

There are currently two dominant frameworks guiding efforts to integrate technology in most school systems: TPACK (Technological, Pedagogical, and Content Knowledge) and SAMR (Substitution, Augmentation, Modification, and Redefinition). Both TPACK and SAMR will be described further in Chapter 2. However, these models only peripherally address the essential question, and because they lack the necessary organizational structures, such as clear indicators, incremental stages, clear transitions, and instructional strategies, these models can be easily misinterpreted and misapplied. In this book, I introduce a new model: the T3 Framework, which is designed to provide more precise, timely, and actionable feedback to guide educational technology use. A comparison of the elements of TPACK, SAMR, and the T3 Framework is shown in Table P.1.

TABLE P.1 ■ Comparison of the TPACK, SAMR, and T3 Models

Attribute	TPACK	SAMR	T3
Research-based framework	✓	✓	✓
Unambiguous	✓	✓	✓
Contextualized in teaching and learning	✓		✓
Hierarchical		✓	✓
Unambiguous stages			✓
Unambiguous transitions			✓
Design questions			✓
Actionable			✓
Highly reliable instructional strategies			✓
Clear indicators of progress			✓
Can be used to set clear professional growth goals			✓
Can be used to measure progress on growth goals			✓
Can be used to track progress on growth goals			✓

Note: Check marks indicate a positive correlation with any given attribute.

Table P.1 shows that the TPACK and SAMR technology integration models do not contain many of the attributes necessary to address the essential question. The T3 model does by intentional design. Of particular note is the use of incremental stages that can be used to identify one's current use of technology, guide appropriate action for improvement, and measure progress. For example, TPACK and SAMR present ordinal stages using terms such as *technological knowledge* and *modification*. Linguistic stages are more open to ambiguity, misinterpretation, and error, which increases the difficulty in identifying, measuring, and tracking progress within and between stages. The T3 Framework incorporates both ordinal and nominal or numerical stages to mitigate this ambiguity and the introduction of error. Moreover, the T3 model is informed by two critical premises:

1. Technology use should unleash student learning potential in ways that are not possible in the absence of technology.

2. Education systems would benefit from a taxonomy of the value added by technology use in learning environments, which would result in more impactful teaching practices and increased student engagement and achievement.

These two dominant themes have guided my professional practice as an educator and researcher, and serve as the foundation for this book.

ORGANIZATION OF THIS BOOK

This book is an attempt to positively disrupt the current narrative about educational technology use in learning systems. I hope to do so by introducing a new framework, the T3 Framework, into the dialogue of how to use digital tools for schools. The T3 Framework is a continuum that represents the increasing value add of technology by framing the use of educational technologies in our classrooms in three distinct stages of use: translational, transformational, and transcendent. These three distinct stages increment the value added by the use of educational technologies, from low to high, to support maximizing the return on the investment of technology specifically within the context of modern teaching and learning. This book offers educational leaders and classroom teachers the structure, strategies, and tools for infusing transcendent uses of technology into their schools, classrooms, and daily lessons.

Chapter 1 begins with a discussion of disruptive innovation, why it is a positive force for change, and how schools can manage disruptive transitions.

Chapter 2 is a review of some current technology integration frameworks, and their strengths and their weaknesses, and concludes with a brief overview of the T3 Framework and the translational, transformational, and transcendent stages of technology use.

The next section includes a more detailed explanation of each stage of the T3 Framework. Chapter 3 discusses the most common type of educational technology use: translational. In the translational stage of technology use, teachers and students use technologies to do digitally what they once did using analog tools. The two incremental steps of translational technology are automation and consumption. While these steps do add value, the value added is comparatively low.

Chapter 4 provides an overview of the second stage of technology integration: transformational technology use. When digital tools are used in a transformational way, both the task itself and the agent engaged in the task are substantively changed by the use of technology. The two incremental steps in the transformational stage are production and contribution.

Chapter 5 begins with a discussion of transcendent technology use and why it is imperative that educational systems embrace the transcendent use of technology to push the limits of current educational outcomes. The two steps of transcendent technology use are inquiry design and social entrepreneurship. In addition to providing the highest value for technology use in schools, these two steps go above and beyond the existing range of experiences and expectations of digital tools used in today's classrooms.

The final section of this book includes a discussion on the different ways to apply the T3 Framework. Chapter 6 begins with an overview of how teachers can use the T3 Framework to self-assess how they currently use technology, set goals, and engage in the process of continuous growth and mastery. This is followed by a discussion of how the T3 Framework can be used both to guide and to inform modern teacher evaluations. The chapter concludes with a discussion of how the T3 Framework can be used to facilitate professional and organizational development for classroom teachers and school, district, and state leaders.

It is my sincere hope that through the application of the T3 Framework in our classrooms, we can collectively identify the synergies—the "sweet spots"—where technology most reliably supports, augments, and enhances the quality of classroom teaching and learning. For more than 30 years, I have endeavored to help educators use digital tools to generate their own disruptive classroom innovations that put student thinking, knowledge generation, and knowledge representation at the core of their instructional practice. I believe that this ethos will support the service of improving teaching and learning for our students here and now, and well into the future.

Introduction

1 A CASE FOR DISRUPTIVE INNOVATION IN EDUCATION

Ever tried? Ever failed? No matter.

Try again. Fail again. Fail *better*.

—Samuel Beckett

WHAT IS DISRUPTIVE INNOVATION?

Life and work in the 21st century clearly demand new learning outcomes for students. This means that in addition to the traditional literacies necessary for success, today's students must continuously develop mastery of new knowledge, skills, competencies, aptitudes, and literacies that were not requisite for college and career success in the 20th century. Education has decidedly entered a period of profound disruptive transition. The disruptive innovation train has left the station; however, not everyone is in their seats, or even on board.

One reason may be affect: Many people feel that disruption is a negative force. We don't like being disrupted, whether we are watching television, reading a book, or strumming a guitar. On the whole, we would rather avoid disruptions if we can help it.

> Life and work in the 21st century clearly demand new learning outcomes for students.

Disruption may invoke such negativity because it presupposes change—a change between the status quo and some new reality. Even the term *change* can evoke a negative visceral reaction. Change requires the investment of one's discretionary energy, something not everyone will do freely, because we take great comfort in our routines. To willingly step outside of our comfortable routines, we must first perceive a significant return on the investment of our discretionary energy.

The term *disruption*, particularly in the context of the classroom, has been given a bad rap over the years. When one thinks about a disruptive classroom, one envisions every teacher's nightmare: a group of misbehaving students who are completely beyond the influence of their teacher, a class spiraling out of control. While disruption is an uncomfortable proposition in general, disruption in education is even more discomforting given the enormous complexities and variability inherent in the processes of teaching and learning.

Changing the routines and procedures to which educators have become accustomed is exceedingly discomforting—particularly if one achieves a level of success with practices that have withstood the test of time and from which one realizes acceptable results. It is understandable that teachers will fill their pedagogical toolboxes with methods that have had demonstrable reliability over the years, and that the longer they have used such practices, the more reluctant they will be to disrupt or relinquish them.

So why add to the infinite complexities of a classroom full of students by introducing something that is disruptive? To explore that further, let's first rethink the connotations of the word *disruption*. Clayton Christensen and his colleagues (Christensen, Horn, & Johnson, 2008) succinctly summarize that which, for many of us, is a confounding contradiction in terms: "Disruption is a positive force. It is the process by which an innovation transforms a market whose services or products are complicated and expensive into one where simplicity, convenience, accessibility, and affordability characterize the industry" (p. 11).

Christensen et al. (2008) go a step further by offering a new theory—disruptive innovation theory. Unlike sustaining innovations, which are characterized by confusion, obscurity, and a high level of complexity, disruptive innovations are not necessarily breakthrough improvements in processes or procedures. Rather, disruptive innovations are easy to understand. They make sense because they fall easily within our existing paradigm. They seem self-evident. They are manageable, accessible, and not so far out of the range of our current practices or procedures to make them "too far out" for general consideration and widespread adoption (Christensen et al., 2008).

For example, Christensen and colleagues (2008) suggest that the Apple II computer was a disruptive innovation. Personal computers, at the time, were large, cumbersome, and arguably complicated from a user's perspective. Rather than compete with IBM's firm hold on the personal computer market, Apple marketed the Apple II not as a personal computer but as a toy. It even looked like a toy, with the friendly interface and now iconic smiling computer icon. To the novice user, computers were intimidating, but toys weren't. The Apple II wasn't necessarily a breakthrough in computing power, speed, or storage. Instead, it was easy to understand and easy to use. As a result, the Apple II became widely adopted and used in homes, businesses, and most important to our topic at hand, schools (Christensen et al., 2008).

MANAGING DISRUPTIVE TRANSITIONS IN EDUCATION

The Apple II was a "toy" that, in the fall of 1984, when I was a young grad student at Rutgers University, disrupted my earliest thoughts about teaching and learning with technology. But could the introduction of the Apple II in education be considered a disruptive innovation, or was it a distraction from effective instruction? The answer, which I've come to after more than 30 years of failing better, is this: Educational technologies can be either a disruptive innovation or distractive innovation; the dependent variable seems to be the manner in which the technology is used.

One of the first educational technology studies I conducted involved determining the effect of the Apple II on student engagement. Some fellow grad students and I observed and coded the engagement behaviors (low, medium, or high) of a group of local middle school students at the new Rutgers educational computer lab in Camden, New Jersey. The students were to complete the tasks in a recently developed learning program called the Oregon Trail. Students' engagement was consistently high when they first interacted with the program. However, over a relatively short period of time, their engagement level dropped significantly. As students became bored with the program, they were more easily distracted and began seeking other behaviorally disruptive ways to sustain their interest levels.

Because the technology was so new to education, our early research followed a "let's add the technology and see what happens" mindset. The "novelty effect" I first observed in 1984 presaged a predictable pattern: One can expect a short-term increase in student interest and engagement due to the novelty of the technology experience, but because novelty is unsustainable, one can also expect to see a precipitous drop in student interest, engagement, and performance. As new technologies have emerged and been placed in schools over the past 30 years, we've seen the roller coaster of student engagement and performance rise and fall, going up after the addition of some new technologies—the Internet, the World Wide Web, laptops, handheld computers, interactive whiteboards, tablets—and coming back down after the novelty of that technology has worn off.

Former Stanford professor Larry Cuban and his colleagues (Cuban, Kirkpatrick, & Peck, 2001) studiously observed that computers have historically been treated as add-ons to traditional classroom practices. Instead of bringing about innovative disruptions, computers were relegated to the back of the classroom, where students could play games (like the Oregon Trail) as a reward for completing their classwork (Cuban et al., 2001). The commonality of low-value use of technology is hardly cause for celebration.

This pattern has played out over and over again in classrooms where technology is added in a manner that reflects high optimism but low intentionality.

Breaking out of this cycle of distractive innovation with technology will allow our schools to engage in sustainable methods that reliably improve instructional quality and student learning performance.

Frustratingly, while many supporters and critics of public education have described the need to change our system of teaching and learning, many fail to adequately explain exactly what we should be doing differently. We've answered the question of why we need classroom technologies; now we need to address the question of how we use technologies to meet the needs of third millennium students. This may not be so easy to articulate, but the indicators of knowledge generation and knowledge representation—what we want students to know and be able to do, and how they might demonstrate what they know and are able to do—absolutely must be reflective of the digital contexts in which they live. This may provide some stable means of ascertaining how schools in the future might look.

With that future in mind, we must first help school systems begin to transition between low-value uses of digital tools to higher-value uses. This process naturally requires tending to the change process itself, as well as managing the transitions between the ending of some old practices and the tentative steps toward implementing new ones.

To fail better, as Samuel Beckett counsels, education must let go of the false hope of technological determinism: the notion that simply having access to educational technologies will automatically lead to disruptive innovations and gains in student learning performance. To break the cycle, we need to first understand the principles and practices that constitute effective pedagogical practice. A brief overview of these principles and practices follows.

PRINCIPLES OF EFFECTIVE PEDAGOGY

A reasonable starting point for a review of effective pedagogical methods in schools may be found in two singular theoretical principles: John Dewey's (1938) principles of continuity and interaction. Dewey was a progressive educator who was well ahead of his time, and his principle of continuity suggests that the totality of one's past experiences is carried forward and exerts an influence on current and future decisions and experiences. In other words, one's past knowledge and experience are the foundation on which all new knowledge is constructed.

Dewey's principle of interaction refers to the conditional relationship among the learner, the new content information the learner experiences, and the environment in which that interaction takes place (Dewey, 1938). The principle of interaction suggests that learning is an active rather than a passive process. A disruptor in his own right, Dewey roundly rejected the idea that students were empty vessels that their teachers filled with the magical elixir of knowledge, the predominant pedagogical sentiment at the time. Dewey taught us that, rather than sitting quietly and passively absorbing new information, learners need to create connections between new information and their previously actualized knowledge base by interacting with that new information in meaningful ways within meaningful contexts. To support the interactive nature of knowledge generation, learning environments need to be highly participatory places where students can experientially and playfully build relationships between and among new information, their prior knowledge, their teacher, one another, and their own reflective understandings. Learning is not only a team sport but a contextual team sport.

These two principles, while distinct, are both highly correlated and underscore critical components of any pedagogical context, past or present. It would be worthwhile to consider applying the principles of continuity and interaction, not only as they relate to an individual student but as they relate to the micro context of the learning environment in which the student is effectively generating knowledge connections and the macro context, or the larger societal context in which the learning environment itself exists. The knowledge and experiences gained by students in classroom learning environments not only are impacted by learners' unique backgrounds and interests but also must be reflective of the knowledge, skills, competencies, and aptitudes needed to thrive in the world outside of that classroom.

> The knowledge and experiences gained by students in classroom learning environments not only are impacted by learners' unique backgrounds and interests but also must be reflective of the knowledge, skills, competencies, and aptitudes needed to thrive in the world outside of that classroom.

Modern perspectives on the environmental conditions that are most conducive to supporting and enhancing human cognition have a solid grounding in the theoretical and empirical research literature on learning. Eminent researcher John Bransford and his colleagues (Bransford, Brown, & Cocking, 2000) build on Dewey's progressive learning principles by identifying five principles that could be regarded as essential to modern interactive and participatory teaching and learning. These five principles are listed in Table 1.1.

TABLE 1.1 ■ Modern Pedagogical Principles

1. Learning builds on previous experiences.

2. Learning is a social activity.

3. New content information should be framed within meaningful contexts.

4. New content information should be connected, organized, and relevant.

5. Feedback and active evaluation enhance the learning process.

Source: Adapted from Bransford et al. (2000).

The cumulative experience that students bring to the learning moment is the foundation on which all new knowledge is constructed. It's imperative, then, that teachers activate this prior knowledge as often as possible to help students build connections and explore the myriad relationships between what they already know and the new content they are experiencing. Activating and building students' background knowledge is a foundational principle for modern learning (Marzano, 2004).

It may not be too far of a stretch to suggest that learning experiences can be optimized by the process of discussing our tentative understanding of new content knowledge with someone who is more knowledgeable than ourselves. This may be part of our genetic heritage as social animals who are genetically predisposed to vast learning capacity (Morris, 1968). Constructivist learning theory suggests that it is through discussion that knowledge and meaning are constructed. To practice and deepen newly acquired content information, learners greatly benefit from engaging in learning tasks that allow them to talk about new information, reflect on that information, and engage in collaborative problem-solving or investigative tasks in which that new information is applied (Vygotsky, 1978).

Humans use language to construct knowledge and representations of what we know, what we are able to do, and how we think about our learning. To make sense of new information within the classroom context, students must interact discursively with their peers. Modern learners need to talk about new content information to fit that information into their current knowledge base. This is a dynamic process that requires students to reflect on how they think about new information, as well as to generate and test tentative claims about that information individually and collaboratively (Magana & Marzano, 2014a; Marzano, 2007).

Contextualizing new content information within a meaningful framework grounds the learning experience for students by adding numerous options for connecting prior knowledge to new knowledge. Putting new content information into a meaningful context helps learners make sense of how the new information they are experiencing is connected to past as well as future content knowledge. Presenting new content knowledge in the absence of a meaningful context confuses students and inhibits their ability to construct understanding and meaning.

New content information needs to be connected, organized in a logical sequence, and relevant to the larger environment in which students live. This helps students not only build connections between their foundational knowledge and new content information but also improve their understanding of and interactions with themselves and the world around them. Never has this been truer than in our modern, globalized society (Magana & Marzano, 2014a).

One of the most reliable ways to increase learning performance is to improve the quality and quantity of learning feedback. Continuous feedback in the learning process should provide learners with three critical pieces of information: (1) a clear understanding of the learning objective, (2) an estimation of their proximity to achieving proficiency with the learning objective, and (3) an awareness of the strategies and tasks they must enact to achieve the learning objective (Hattie, 2009; Magana & Marzano, 2014a; Marzano, 2007; Marzano, Pickering, & Pollock, 2001).

PRINCIPLES OF EFFECTIVE TECHNOLOGY INTEGRATION

Effective classroom instruction, however, does not occur in a vacuum. The advent of a highly globalized and technologized environment, the macro context, demands that new digital tools be wielded effectively for classroom environments, the micro context, to remain connected, meaningful, and relevant. But should we focus on the pedagogy or the technology?

If you've ever listened closely to the iconic song "Because" on the album *Abbey Road*, then you will recognize this song as having one of the Beatles' most beautiful vocal arrangements (Lennon & McCartney, 1970). The foundation is the melody, as sung by John Lennon. However, when that melody is enhanced by George Harrison's low and Paul McCartney's high harmonies, the song becomes transcendent; it becomes music of the highest order. Listening to either the melody or harmonies alone would inestimably diminish the listening experience. A good melody enhanced by good harmonies results in great music. This is an apt metaphor for effective teaching and learning with technology: Good teaching is the melody, and good technology integration adds the harmony, resulting in greater impact. The whole is greater than the sum of its parts.

We must also consider the fact that today's modern learners begin interacting with multisensory touchscreens at a very early age. So does this level of multisensory interaction in virtual environments have a positive impact on a child's readiness to learn? Perhaps. However, an argument could be made that the virtual environment alone, the digital context, is insufficient as a means of bringing about authentic learning and understanding. Without the meaningful guidance and support of an effective teacher, children's interaction with technology tends to be predominantly banal and trivial (McFarlane, 2015).

> Good teaching is the melody, and good technology integration adds the harmony, resulting in greater impact.

Much of what is currently known about improving a learner's interaction with knowledge has been well established in the research literature. For example, the inclusion of visual or nonlinguistic representations of ideas and new knowledge helps improve how effectively students interact with new knowledge. Richard Mayer's (2001) findings from quantitative studies with graduate students suggest that learners learn more from pictures and words than from either pictures without words or words without pictures. This dual-coding theory, that learners make better sense of new content through words and pictures, is at the heart of Mayer's (2001) findings. Today, however, if one were to add the tactile-powered interactivity of current touchscreen technologies, one could reasonably argue that such experiences might enhance not only a child's interaction with that new knowledge but also the child's natural inclination to generate and test inferences about that entire experience. One can imagine a child's inner dialogue along the lines of, *When I touch that image of a cow on the screen, I hear the sound of a cow; so if I touch that image of a kitty on the screen, then I'll hear the sound a kitty makes.* Does this kind of experience demand a new tricoding theory that includes words, images, and tactile interaction with those words and pictures? Perhaps it does.

My friend and coauthor Dr. Robert J. Marzano recently summarized his findings on the impact of technology on student achievement, stating that "a good teacher with technology will usually outperform a good teacher without technology" (Magana & Marzano, 2014b). This is indeed cause for optimism, because taken at face value, compounding research evidence points to a strong trend: Learning environments in which technologies are integrated to enhance multisensory interaction, knowledge expression and representation, discussion, feedback, and reflection improve student learning (Hattie, 2009, 2012; Haystead & Magana, 2013; Haystead & Marzano, 2009, 2010; Magana, 2016; Magana & Marzano, 2014a).

Taking all these premises together, a strong argument can be made that modern technology integration practices should reflect the following principles (see Table 1.2).

TABLE 1.2 ■ Modern Technology Integration Principles

1. A primary focus on implementing highly reliable instructional principles and strategies with fidelity

2. A secondary focus on leveraging readily available technologies to support, augment, and enhance highly reliable instructional principles and strategies with fidelity

3. A tertiary focus on mindfully monitoring the impact of Principles 1 and 2 on students' social and academic performance

Still, effective and systemic technology integration in classroom instruction remains frustratingly elusive. A contributing factor may be that far too many educational software and online learning experiences offer only repetitive "drill-and-practice" learning experiences. When using these technologies, students are reduced to mere passive consumers of decontextualized "facts" that could be delivered as easily by a machine as by a textbook. Such tools are designed to reinforce basic skills through rote memorization in the absence of any meaningful context—precisely the kind of passive learning that Dewey rejected as ineffective nearly 100 years ago.

So how did we get to this unhappy place? The rise of the "digital worksheet" may be another reason for the disappointing impact of educational technologies on student achievement—precisely because it is used as a direct replacement for a human teacher. In regard to the effective use of educational technology, there appear to be two different camps: those who favor technology as a replacement for teachers and those who favor technology as a supplement to a good teacher.

Author Marc Prensky (2001) introduced a metaphor to explain his opinion why, despite large investments for educational technologies in K–12 classrooms, schools in the United States had not realized significant gains in student achievement. Prensky surmised the reason to be that today's students are "digital natives" who use technology as native language speakers while classroom teachers are "digital immigrants" who communicate with a pronounced accent (Prensky, 2001). In his widely circulated paper "Digital Natives, Digital Immigrants," Prensky assertively advocates for replacing teachers with technology and letting the digital natives use computers to teach themselves. He essentially calls for teachers, the digital immigrants, to get out of the way (Prensky, 2001).

John Hattie (2012) disagrees. He suggests that the problem with Prensky's theory of digital nativity is that it is presented in the absence of any evidence. Professor Hattie suggests that Prensky ascribes to children attributes they simply do not possess and therefore his theory should be disregarded because it is "basically incorrect" (Hattie, 2012). Internationally renowned educational technologist Professor Angela McFarlane (2015) also observed that Prensky harbors a kind of "techno-romanticism," which suggests that to realize the potential of educational technologies, they should be used as replacements for classroom teachers (McFarlane, 2015). Professor McFarlane argues that, rather than simply replacing teachers with computers and online content, educational technology tools should be incorporated into the framework of what is currently considered effective instruction:

> In reality much that we know about learning, communicating, creating knowledge and sharing it, remains valid in the face of connected digital technologies. Recognizing this and adapting effective practice to new contexts is at the heart of understanding how digital technologies can best support effective teaching and meaningful, authentic learning. (p. 9)

A final important trend readily emerges from the research literature: When technology tools are used to replace teachers, one can expect a very small to small effect on student academic achievement (Cheung & Slavin, 2011; Hattie, 2009, 2012). When educational technologies are used to supplement teachers' instructional methods, one can expect a moderate effect on student learning (Hattie, 2009, 2012; Haystead & Marzano, 2009, 2010). However, when teachers use technology to enhance highly reliable principles and strategies, one can expect a large to very large effect on student learning (Haystead & Magana, 2013; Haystead & Marzano, 2009, 2010; Magana, 2016; Magana & Marzano, 2014a). The heart of this work is to ensure that educators and educational leaders have the guidance and resources to reliably integrate readily available educational technologies to optimize students' social and academic growth.

SUMMARY

To consider effective pedagogy in the 21st century, one simply must consider the larger environmental context in which that learning takes place. As work and life in this century transform due to increasing globalization and the application of information and communication technologies, so too should modern learning environments reflect these changes. While this has been a desired outcome for the past 30 years, the impact of educational technology tools on student achievement has not matched the potential of these tools to reliably enhance teaching and learning. A contributing element of this problem may be an overemphasis on low-value use of educational technology tools in our schools.

A potential resolution to this problem rests with the development of an actionable framework for educational technology use that primarily emphasizes highly reliable pedagogical principles and strategies, places a secondary emphasis on ways teachers can enhance these principles and practices with their available classroom technologies, and places a tertiary emphasis on monitoring the impact on student social and academic success. This not only will serve to improve student learning outcomes but also will better prepare students for social and professional success in the conceptual economy of the digital age. In the next chapter we will further explore the benefits of frameworks and how the T3 Framework can serve as a guide for reliably increasing student performance by incrementing the value added by technology use in schools.

2 THE T3 FRAMEWORK
A New Framework for Innovation in Education

There are these two young fish swimming along, and they happen
to meet an older fish swimming the other way, who nods at
them and says, "Morning, boys, how's the water?" And the two
young fish swim on for a bit, and then eventually one of them
looks over at the other and goes, "What the hell is water?"

**—David Foster Wallace, commencement
address at Kenyon College, 2005**

THE IMPORTANCE OF FRAMEWORKS

It's helpful to contextualize our thinking about digital innovation in education within a clear framework that is useful and actionable. Just as the struc-
tural framework of a house shapes and defines the whole structure, conceptual
frameworks help us organize complex phe-
nomena so we can make holistic sense out
of the experience. Using frameworks helps
ground our understanding of some new or
disorienting experience so we can generate contextual understanding and engage in
fruitful meaning making (Fairhurst, 2011).
Frameworks also help us see the "big picture"
so we don't end up like the young fish in David
Foster Wallace's (2005) allegory, swimming
around aimlessly without any clue as to the context in which we are swimming.
A meaningful technology integration framework can guide how educators think
about, enact, and communicate educational innovation with technology to more
reliably impact student learning.

> A meaningful technology
> integration framework can
> guide how educators think
> about, enact, and communicate
> educational innovation with
> technology to more reliably
> impact student learning.

However, the reliable integration of educational technologies to enhance teaching and learning could be characterized as a wicked problem (Rittel & Webber, 1973). Wicked problems are those with numerous constraints that keep changing and developing more complications. Wicked problems remind me of the mythic Hydra. Each time you cut one head off the Hydra, several new heads grow in its place. Consistently integrating technology in classrooms is like wrestling the Hydra. So often it seems like when one technology integration element starts working well, several other things go horribly wrong. Such a complex and seemingly intractable problem would be well served by a framework that helps educators innovate their practices with technology to reliably unleash student learning potential.

This book is designed as a solution to this wicked problem by offering a method of contextualizing and evaluating the uses of educational technology tools in a clear framework for improving student engagement and achievement. Supporting educators and instructional leaders who evaluate instructional efficacy with technology will afford students the opportunities to develop the skills, aptitudes, and habits that will serve them as knowledge workers in a conceptual, digital, and global economy.

To put things in perspective, the introduction of educational technology tools in classrooms is a relatively recent phenomenon. The novelty of such a phenomenon naturally engenders different forms of bias (Magana & Marzano, 2014). Before we go any further, ask yourself how you would characterize your "technology bias." Take a few moments to answer the following questions:

- Do you feel frustrated or intimidated when you experience new technologies?
- Do you feel excited or exhilarated when you experience new technologies?
- Do you feel anxiety about adopting new technologies in your classroom?
- Do you feel enthusiastic about adopting new technologies in your classroom?
- Do you feel that technology will automatically add value to your instruction?
- Do you feel that technology will automatically reduce value in your instruction?

Some people subconsciously harbor a value-positive bias toward technology and think that educational technologies will have a positive impact on teaching and learning by their very presence. Those who harbor this bias tend to think of educational technologies as a kind of panacea for the issues that plague public education. Some others hold to a value-negative bias and believe that there is no place for technologies in the modern classroom, whether it's because of the expense, the issues around insufficient or inequitable access, or the challenges with teacher training. People who operate under this bias feel that sufficient gains have been made over the years through tried-and-true (some would say traditional) teaching practices that make educational technology tools superfluous.

My perspective is that educational technology tools really should be characterized as "value neutral." Specifically, educational technology tools have no inherent value in and of themselves. Rather, the value of any educational technology is made manifest by the manner in which it is used to support, augment, or enhance effective instructional practices. It is logical, therefore, to consider that there exists a continuum from low-value to high-value uses for any educational technology tool. Taken at face value, this value-neutral lens may help education professionals take a huge step toward reframing how to consider acquiring and implementing educational technology tools and, perhaps more important, training teachers to use these tools to enhance effective instruction.

It appears that for the past 30 years, educators have viewed technology with either a value-positive bias or a value-negative bias. It is high time for a new way of thinking about educational technology, not through the frame of the inherent value of such tools but by considering the manner in which those technologies are used to generate value in the process of teaching and learning. The increases in readily available educational technologies have also given rise to patterns of disruptive innovation. With educational technology tools, teachers are now able to engage in innovative, highly effective instructional methodologies that are simply not possible without the technology. With nuanced changes in how the tools are used, teachers can achieve innovative disruptions in three critical learning elements:

> Educational technology tools have no inherent value in and of themselves. Rather, the value of any educational technology is made manifest by the manner in which it is used to support, augment, or enhance effective instructional practices.

1. Helping students experience new learning content

2. Helping students build and strengthen connections between background knowledge and new learning content

3. Helping students apply their content knowledge to create models that represent new understanding and meaning

It is time to reframe current and emerging technologies through the prism of effective pedagogy to ensure that optimizing students' learning experiences is our core focus.

EXISTING FRAMEWORKS AND THEIR USEFULNESS

Currently, two models are used predominantly in education to frame the use of technology: the TPACK Model and the SAMR Model. While each has its strengths, each also has its limitations rooted in the broadness or narrowness of both its design and potential applications.

TPACK Model

The TPACK Model was developed by Michigan State University professors Punya Mishra and Matthew J. Koehler (1998) to help provide a framework for including technology in the complex processes of teaching and learning. An acronym for Technological, Pedagogical, and Content Knowledge, the TPACK Model highlights the importance of teachers' technological knowledge as equal to that of both content knowledge and pedagogical knowledge in modern classroom settings (see Figure 2.1). While this may seem self-evident, it is arguably not so.

It is clearly important for teachers to attain high levels of knowledge in their subject-area content. They must also ground their classroom methods in the theoretical research literature and experiential knowledge base of pedagogy to reliably elicit understanding and improve student learning productivity. These two competencies have been around for a long time, and it would be very difficult to argue against the importance of having highly qualified classroom teachers who are skilled not only in their content areas but also in highly reliable instructional practices. However, in an increasingly globalized world economy powered by digital technologies, these two competencies can be considered adequate yet insufficient for preparing youth for a modern world of life and work. The missing competency is technological knowledge, and professors Mishra and Koehler (1998) helped raise the importance of technological knowledge as an inextricable component of effective modern instruction. If one looks at the diagrammatic representation of the TPACK Model in Figure 2.1, one sees that the center of the model is the figurative intersection where modern teachers should set their sights: the confluence of technological knowledge, pedagogical knowledge, and content knowledge. It would be hard to argue against this nexus as the destination for modern educators to reach.

When the TPACK Model made its way into the education system's consciousness, it immediately made sense to many educators, because to be relevant and effective in a modern context, modern teachers needed to use modern tools to teach modern students to prepare the students for an increasingly modernized future. This is a fact that was articulated by my colleague Dr. Robert J. Marzano, who once said to me, "If we don't fully embrace educational technology as an integral part of the process of teaching and learning, then we'll all be dinosaurs" (R. J. Marzano, personal communication, 2010). To say that the TPACK Model helped highlight the importance of teachers' technological knowledge in the narrative of modern instructional quality is an understatement. The extent to which teachers have consistently adopted innovative instructional practices with technology, however, remains tenuous.

FIGURE 2.1 ■ TPACK Model

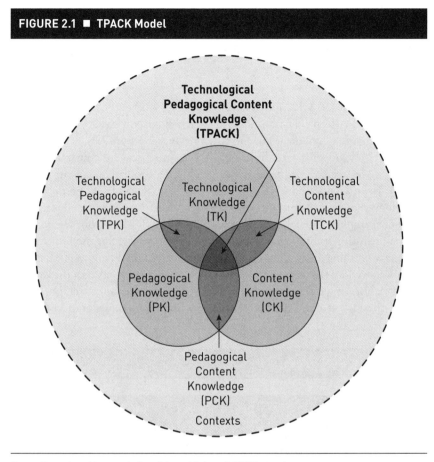

*Source:*Reproduced by permission of the publisher, © 2012 by tpack.org.

This model, however, lacks a thorough elucidation of the steps one might reasonably follow to develop technological knowledge. What are the incremental stages for achieving that goal? What are the processes that educators could reliably follow to achieve technological knowledge and continuously improve on and expand that knowledge base? This is a challenge, because as a teacher, I would do well to know with reasonable precision the overarching goals of "technological knowledge" and have indicators to guide me along my journey. If I am going to set technological knowledge goals for myself, I need to know what it means to have technological knowledge so I can set reasonable goals, determine where I am in relation to those goals, and over time, track my progress toward those goals.

While the TPACK Model does help establish the importance of technological knowledge for teachers, it does not provide any guidance or measurable standards to help teachers attain that knowledge. This makes it harder for teachers to self-assess their current technological knowledge, set meaningful goals, and monitor their progress toward those goals. It also makes it more challenging for administrators to accurately evaluate teachers' technological knowledge.

SAMR Model

More recently, the SAMR Model, developed by Dr. Ruben Puentedura (2013), emerged. The SAMR Model frames the use of technology in four stages: substitution, augmentation, modification, and redefinition (see Figure 2.2).

The SAMR Model is actually a highly conceptual scale or continuum that focuses on the relative degree to which technology tools change the nature of tasks. In this regard, one can consider the SAMR Model to be decidedly technology-centric; so it can be transposed to any purpose, not just educational ones. For example, at the substitution stage of the SAMR Model, one would simply be substituting technology tools for other tools that might be used to accomplish a task, without any improvement regarding functionality of the task itself. This is followed by the augmentation stage of using technology as a direct tool substitute, but the nature of the technology tool adds some functional improvement to the task at hand. In both the substitution and augmentation stages,

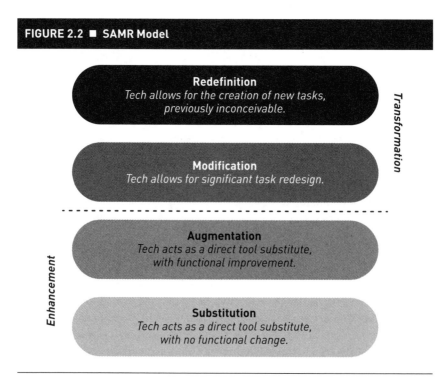

FIGURE 2.2 ■ SAMR Model

Redefinition
Tech allows for the creation of new tasks, previously inconceivable.

Transformation

Modification
Tech allows for significant task redesign.

Augmentation
Tech acts as a direct tool substitute, with functional improvement.

Enhancement

Substitution
Tech acts as a direct tool substitute, with no functional change.

Source: Puentedura (2009).

the use of technology tools can be considered enhancement, because there is some enhancement to the task at hand by using technology but not much.

The third step of the SAMR Model considers that the use of a technology tool allows some significant redesign or modification of the task. The final step is redefinition, the stage at which the use of the technology tool allows for the creation of new tasks that are not possible without the technology tool. Because the use of technology either modifies or redefines the task, these final two stages are considered to be transformational (Puentedura, 2013).

The SAMR Model builds on the TPACK Model by providing a more in-depth hierarchy for categorizing technology tool use. In this regard, it is a helpful organizing framework, but it is entirely technology-centric, which makes the implementation of the SAMR Model in teaching and learning a fairly abstract exercise. This is a shortcoming of the SAMR Model, because while it articulates a conceptual framework for the use of technology tools, there is no clearly defined context for that technology use; the SAMR Model might be just as applicable to teaching, typesetting, or trench digging. As such, a strength of the SAMR Model is its generalizability, but in the pedagogical realm, this is a weakness, because the focus of the model is the technology tool, not pedagogy, and this may lead to confusion or a misapplication of the model in the realm of teaching and learning. This adds an unnecessary extra challenge for teachers who want to frame the use of their technology within the context of effective modern instructional practices.

Both the TPACK and SAMR models are helpful steps forward, because they both underscore the importance of educational technologies as having equal value with pedagogical and content knowledge for the modern educator. As a tool-centric framework, the SAMR Model goes deeper into the realm of technology use but seems to lack incremental identifiers of instructional or learning practice that would help meaningfully and accurately guide educators toward higher levels of innovative teaching and learning practices.

So what do I mean when I say disruptive innovation in education? Which classroom practices are transforming teaching and learning? Which practices should be disrupted and why? What does transformation look like? How will you know when transformation has taken place? These are important questions for the reader to keep in mind, as the T3 Framework is a lens through which educators and education stakeholders can determine the differences between low-value and high-value uses of educational technologies in our classrooms, as they relate to learning. The three stages of the T3 model reflect this value-add continuum: translational technology use, transformational technology use, and transcendent technology use (see Figure 2.3).

This idea is rooted in my experience of learning to play the guitar. In the early 1970s, I frequently listened to rock-and-roll radio stations. Inspired, I started teaching myself to play the guitar and became quite proficient at reproducing the songs I heard. I was happy with my progress over the next few years and kept adding new chords to my repertoire, but I didn't think much about my guitar playing in terms of progressing as a musician. I just kept playing the same songs over and over.

One afternoon I heard Eddie Van Halen's guitar solo on the song "Eruption" (Van Halen, 1978). I'd never heard anything like it and immediately went out and bought *Van Halen I*. One could call Eddie a transcendent guitar player, because his use of electric guitar technology was not only disruptive and innovative but clearly far above the range of any musical expression that existed.

A few months later, I happened upon a radio interview with Eddie Van Halen, who was talking about his approach to playing the electric guitar. The interviewer asked him if there was any advice he would give to budding guitarists, and what Eddie said next was something I would never forget. He explained that one might be at the stage characterized by playing and singing songs around a campfire. But, he cautioned, we couldn't improve by continuing to play the same songs again and again. If we wanted to get better, we had to be aware of a second stage of playing through which all great guitarists had to progress: the Chuck Berry stage. He said to become better musicians, we had to play all of Chuck Berry's great guitar licks, learning them like the backs of our hands. Only after mastering that second stage could a guitarist enter the stage where he or she creates a completely new and innovative style of playing.

That 5-minute interview stayed with me for the rest of my life. Eddie Van Halen artfully described a framework for applying disruptive innovation to guitar playing. As a practitioner, I knew that was what I had been missing; I needed some hierarchy to help guide my growth and development and some criteria through which to gain feedback on my progress. Eddie established a three-tiered hierarchy that made perfect sense to me instantly, which is why his guitar-playing framework satisfies the definition of a disruptive innovation. It was not so far out of reach that I considered it too advanced for meaningful consideration, nor was it too simplistic for meaningful consideration. It was completely self-evident.

I designed the T3 Framework to apply what I have learned about the value of frameworks to the process of integrating technology in teaching and learning.

THE T3 FRAMEWORK

T3 is a framework through which we can implement three different domains of educational technology use: translational, transformational, and transcendent. Translational uses of technology simply enable tasks that can be done in an analog or nondigital way to be done digitally. This is rather analogous to the task of translating from one language to another—say English to Spanish. The substance of the communication remains intact, yet the language in which the communication is rendered changes to a different communicative form. The benefits that technology brings to translating an analog experience to a digitized one

FIGURE 2.3 ■ T3 Framework

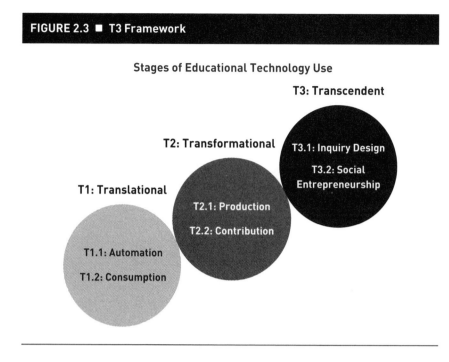

Stages of Educational Technology Use

T3: Transcendent

T2: Transformational

T3.1: Inquiry Design

T3.2: Social Entrepreneurship

T1: Translational

T2.1: Production

T2.2: Contribution

T1.1: Automation

T1.2: Consumption

typically manifest as increases in the speed at which a task is completed, the ease of completing the task, or the accuracy of whoever is performing the task. In terms of teaching and learning, translational uses of technology can be regarded as doing old tasks in new ways—changing tasks from their analog incarnation to a digital one. For example, teachers might distribute a Google form to their students instead of administering a pencil-and-paper survey.

Transformational uses of technology, on the other hand, involve substantive disruptions or changes in either the nature of the task itself, the role of the individual engaged in the task, or the impact of the task on those who perceive the object of the task. This might be analogous to the evolution of human language development from grunts and utterances to pictures of objects to phonemes representing sounds, groups of phonemes creating words, and strings of words creating syntax and structure. Each transformation in the development of how humans communicate was enabled by powerfully disruptive technologies that altered the fundamental substance of the object and task of communication. In terms of teaching and learning, transformational uses of technology can be viewed as doing new things in new ways. The benefits that such transformations bring about are substantive changes in the task itself, the performance of the task, and the performer of the task. History is filled with examples of how the introduction of a disruptive innovation enabled profound innovations that have changed the course of human history. Some examples are the use of fire, the invention of the wheel, the cultivation of crops and the rise of the agrarian society, the forging of metal into tools, the Gutenberg printing press, the development of cell theory and the understanding of pathology, and the introduction of the horse to the Plains Indians. The powerfully disruptive force of innovative technologies causing dramatic changes in human life enabled each of these transformational stories.

Digital technologies now have the potential to take the story of humanity to new and unforeseen heights—to transcendent experiences that go far above and beyond the normal range of expectations and experience. In the world of teaching and learning, digital technologies provide an opportunity for entirely new processes, not just in translating and transforming tasks but transcending what is currently known about teaching and learning with new and emerging technologies that allow us to reach previously unobtainable heights. This is the hallmark of transcendent technology use.

In addition to substantively changing both the task and the agent (the teacher of the learner), transcendent uses of technology go beyond the normal range of expectations of use and practice. For perhaps the first time in human history, learners of all ages can create new learning environments and design new learning tools through the application of software coding. Today's students clearly have the potential, then, to achieve levels of mastery and design that go well above and beyond the typical learning expectations and objectives of knowledge gain. However, with the advent of 3D printing, learners of all ages now have the added ability to make things, to manufacture tools or objects that satisfy a need, solve a problem, or create entirely new ways of doing things. "Maker clubs" have sprung up in pockets across the country as these technologies have become more available and less expensive.

Rather than relegating such uses of technology to after-school clubs or off-campus programs, as is typical in schools with little or no room in their curricula for content that is not assessed with high-stakes (and low-value) testing, I strongly suggest that all students be given an equal opportunity to experience transcendent technology use. As in my guitar-playing analogy, often when one simply becomes aware that higher categories of expertise exist, one is more likely to adjust or raise one's goals to new heights. The T3 Framework is such a set of categories to help education systems "thaw" by reexamining current practices in the face of new technologies, moving forward to new innovative practices, and then "refreezing" into a new state of practices (Lewin, 1947). Educational systems need to embrace this type of organizational development as an iterative process rather than a singular occurrence.

While translational uses of technology provide the lowest level of value to the instructional or learning task, one is bound to remain in this category if one is simply not aware of other, more advanced categories of technology use. As most teacher trainings on using computers in classrooms have generally been focused on enabled translational tasks of instruction and learning, the predominant use of technologies in our classrooms is translational in nature. This is certainly a factor contributing to the limited impact that computers, laptops, tablets, software, and computer-based learning have had on teaching and learning. In fact, one could argue that despite billions of dollars spent cramming computers into classrooms, in terms of substantive changes in teaching and learning, we have very little to show for this investment.

The fundamental problem is an overabundance of translational technology use and very little transformative or transcendent technology use. This book attempts to resolve this problem by providing educators and education stakeholders with a new framework through which they can think about their own use of technology in terms of the low, medium, or high value the technology use provides the learner. This "value-add" taxonomy, then, may provide teachers with specific feedback to help them self-assess and become more deeply reflective of their own use of technology and then plan for increasing the level of innovation. The value of such rigorous reflection, directly in terms of instructional quality, student engagement, and student achievement, is high.

One can consider the T3 Framework as a disruptive innovation framework or continuum, in that one will constantly move between the levels in this framework. This will occur quite naturally, as there will be times during the instructional day when the educational technology tools will be used to solve temporal or administrative constraints or problems. At other times, teachers will simply wish to gain the most value from their instructional uses of technology.

The T3 Framework can also be used as a framework for principals and instructional leaders to evaluate teachers' instructional prowess with educational technology. Ideally, this process should be used for both measurement and developmental purposes. Right now there are no tools to help evaluators readily and reliably consider teachers' use of educational technology tools. This may be a key obstacle impeding the systemic integration of technology in teaching and learning in our classrooms.

The T3 Framework can also be considered a guide for purchasing educational technologies. Instructional coaches can also use this framework to ascertain teachers' instructional gaps and develop coaching plans to help build teachers' capacity with greater specificity. Decision makers need to have some guidance to realize their fiduciary responsibility as managers of public funds. Such decision makers can view potential educational technology tools through the T3 Framework to help determine the value-add proposition for any educational technology purchase. When designing instructional spaces, architects and school design professionals can also use the framework to help them think about the nature of the learning that will take place in those spaces, with an eye toward transformational and transcendent teaching and learning practices in the instructional space. Finally, but not least important, the T3 Framework can also be used as a guide to help policy makers think differently about school transformation by crafting policy through the lens of modern instructional practices that engender consistently high learning outcomes.

SUMMARY

We examined two existing frameworks in this chapter: the TPACK Model and the SAMR Model. Both have been helpful in terms of raising the specter of technology as a necessary component of modern instruction and offering a hierarchy of technology uses. However, neither model sufficiently delineates a process for attaining technological knowledge or higher levels of technology use. The absence of any criteria, incremental indicators, or instructional strategies to guide educators and education systems has led to confusion, misinterpretation, and misapplication of these models.

The T3 Framework was introduced as a new way to frame how we think about innovative technology use in education. The three stages of the T3 model are translational technology use, transformational technology use, and transcendent technology use. The T3 Framework is designed to do three things: (1) necessitate the integration of digital tools in modern teaching and learning, (2) provide a hierarchy of value for the use of technology within the context of learning environments, and (3) offer a set of criteria to help teachers self-assess their current technology use while guiding the process of developing meaningful goals and receiving feedback on the way toward those goals.

The next section will provide a more in-depth discussion of each of the stages and substages of the T3 Framework. We begin with the T1 stage: translational technology use.

Stages of the T3 Framework

3 T1: TRANSLATIONAL TECHNOLOGY USE

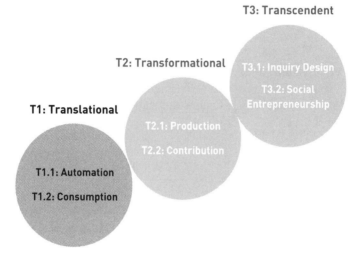

T3: Transcendent

T2: Transformational

T3.1: Inquiry Design

T3.2: Social Entrepreneurship

T1: Translational

T2.1: Production

T2.2: Contribution

T1.1: Automation

T1.2: Consumption

Insanity: Doing the same thing over and over
again and expecting different results.

—Unknown, often attributed to Albert Einstein

TRANSLATIONAL TECHNOLOGY USE DEFINED

Translation can be thought of as the act of transferring or bearing something or some task across two different temporal modalities. We most often think of translation in terms of language. When we translate a message from one language into another, we are really transferring a method of generating meaning, such that the intent of the original message remains intact when converted into a different language. It's like playing your favorite song on a guitar; ideally, the song remains the same.

Changing or altering the meaning or intent of the original message between modalities is not a desirable characteristic of the translation phase, although it does happen. Subtle changes in tone or affect render nuanced shifts in the original message, potentially influencing the interpretation of the delivered message. The less this occurs, however, the stronger the common language experience, which serves to deepen mutual understanding.

> When one engages in translational technology use, one is actually translating tasks or experiences from an analog modality to a digital modality.

Without question, there is value in translating knowledge across media or modalities, and this is an apt analogy for the translational use of digital technologies. However, we must be cautious and keep in mind that, while translational uses of technology provide value, that value is relatively low in comparison with other uses. When one engages in translational technology use, one is actually translating tasks or experiences from an analog modality to a digital modality. The two stages of translational technology use are automation and consumption, discussed in further detail in this chapter.

T1.1: AUTOMATION AND T1.2: CONSUMPTION

As discussed earlier, the two steps of translational technology use in education are T1.1: Automation and T1.2: Consumption. Both these levels mark the translational steps of applying educational technologies to administrative, instructional, or learning tasks. This is primarily how educational technology tools are used in schools and may contribute to why we have not seen systemic transformational use of technology in the process of teaching and learning. It's important to note that the educational technologies discussed in the following section can also be used in ways that add even more value.

So what does translational use of technology in our classrooms look like? Think of a learning task that can be done in a digital mode instead of an analog mode—say, having students use a laptop and word-processing software to write a comparative essay instead of using a pencil and paper. This task is accomplished with little change in substance or form regarding either the task itself or the person accomplishing the task. There is value to digitizing the task, but the value lies with the level of automaticity the technology brings, which illustrates the first stage of the T3 Framework: automation.

T1.1: Automation

Automation can be considered a first step in the value-add continuum of technology use. Automation is the step where either the teacher or the student uses technology to automate, or add varying levels of automation, to instructional or learning tasks. Translating tasks from an analog to a digital mode adds value in terms of saving time, increasing efficiency, and improving accuracy. Computer technologies have allowed humans to make extraordinarily complicated computations at the click of a button. Decisions that previously took a great deal of time and individual effort now take a fraction of a second due to the computing power and automaticity of digital computational tools. Automation is valuable to the user, but in the context of teaching and learning, automation really should be considered an entry-level step. Using educational technology tools to automate tasks or make them easier to accomplish, while useful, offers the lowest value add the technology can bring to a learning environment.

Perhaps a helpful way for educators to consider whether their technology use represents the automation stage is to ask some clarifying questions. The questions and value indicators shown in Table 3.1 help identify the indicators of the automation stage of technology use.

TABLE 3.1 ■ T1.1: Automation—Guiding Questions for Translational Technology Use		
Guiding Question	**Response**	**Value Indicator**
1. Does the technology use result in a time savings?	Yes No	Efficiency
2. Does the technology use result in fewer task-related errors?	Yes No	Accuracy
3. Does the technology use increase the number of tasks completed in a given amount of time?	Yes No	Quantity
4. Does the technology use improve the attributes of the task's end product?	Yes No	Quality

If your answers to these questions are yes, then the technology use you are considering probably aligns with the automation stage. This is the most common way educational technologies are used in our classrooms. While many might perceive this to be a disappointing finding, if one sees this as the first stage of a journey, then it is really cause for renewed optimism, since every teacher and student needs to be using technology in the automation phase. Just remember Eddie Van Halen's advice: You can keep doing what you're doing in the stage you are in, but if you want to get better, you are going to have to go through a transformative phase!

Table 3.2 lists examples of the translational uses of common educational technology tools at the automation level. The tasks, tools, and their relative value add are also listed.

The most common ways technology tools are used in education are in the service of automating the various non-instructional tasks teachers perform on

TABLE 3.2 ■ Common Uses of Educational Technology for Automation of Tasks

Task	Commonly Used Tools	User	Value Add
Document creation and sharing	Microsoft Word Google Drive Microsoft Office 365	Administrators, teachers, students	Time saving, increased efficiency, accuracy, and quantity and quality of documents created
Communicating with other teachers, administrators, or parents	E-mail services	Administrators, teachers, students	Time saving, increased efficiency
Investigating and researching	Google Wikipedia Yahoo Bing	Teachers and students	Time saving, increased efficiency, and access to information sources
Presenting new content information	Google Drive Microsoft PowerPoint Microsoft 365 Interactive Whiteboard Software Prezi Haiku	Teachers	Time saving, increased efficiency, accuracy, quantity of presentations created, and quality of presentations
Testing	Online testing environments	Students	Time saving, increased efficiency, and quantity of test items delivered to students
Grading	Digital gradebook programs Online Learning Management Systems	Teachers	Time saving, increased efficiency, and accuracy
Calculating and budgeting	Microsoft Excel Google Docs Microsoft 365	Administrators, teachers, and students	Time saving, increased efficiency, and accuracy

Source: Adapted from National Education Association (2008).

a regular or daily basis. These tasks are certainly important but are indirectly connected to the process of teaching and learning. Chief among these tasks is teachers' use of computers to increase the speed, efficiency, or accuracy of administrative tasks, such as creating documents, using e-mail to communicate with colleagues, or using the Internet to help plan and prepare for instruction. Of late, however, students' use of computer-based examinations has been a rapidly growing translational use of technology in schools. While these types of tasks are necessary to maintain the administrative functions of the school or the classroom, they should be considered ancillary to tasks that directly address content instruction.

It may be useful to unpack the ways you think about and use digital tools to automate administrative or routine tasks. This is part of the process of reflecting on the "here and now" of your practices with technology, and the available resources in your classroom or school. Answer the questions in Framing Tool T1.1 on the next page to help you think about how you use technology in your teaching, and be sure to notice the picture that emerges.

All the examples of educational technology in the automation step of the framework add value to the teaching and learning experience, but only at the entry level. There is absolutely nothing wrong with this first stage of development, because everybody has to go through it. But it is important to remember that it is only the first stage in the T3 Framework. To improve, one has to go through the next step of development within the domain of translation—consumption—the step at which teachers and students consume media in a digital realm. Let's take a look at some examples of educational technology use for consumption.

T1.2: Consumption

The second step in the T1 stage is using digital technologies to consume information in a digital medium. Let's define consumption in the context of education as the task of accessing some digital form of content-related information or knowledge. One could consider the consumption of content-related information to be of slightly more value than general automation tasks because of the potential digital media have to provide multiple means of representing knowledge. This can include the consumption of any type of media that exists, whether textual, auditory, visual, or in some combined multimedia format. Digitally accessing and consuming media builds on the value added by the automation step in that, in addition to the automaticity afforded by using digital tools for routine tasks, information can be consumed in a variety of ways that stimulate multiple senses simultaneously. So much information is available digitally, through any device and an Internet connection, that learners can consume content-related text, images, sounds, moving images, or any combination therein. The difference is that the consumption of such content has been readily translated from an analog to a digitized form.

FRAMING TOOL T1.1
AUTOMATION

1. What are the digital tools you use to automate tasks on a regular basis?

   _____

   _____

   _____

   _____

2. What are the tasks to which you apply these tools?

   _____

   _____

   _____

   _____

3. How does the use of these tools add value?

   _____

   _____

   _____

   _____

4. What other tasks do you think might be enhanced by digital automation tools?

   _____

   _____

   _____

   _____

Available for download at **www.corwin.com/disruptiveclassroomtech**

Copyright © 2017 by Corwin. All rights reserved. Reprinted from *Disruptive Classroom Technologies: A Framework for Innovation in Education* by Sonny Magana. Thousand Oaks, CA: Corwin, www.corwin.com. Reproduction authorized only for the local school site or nonprofit organization that has purchased this book.

The step of consuming information is important for teachers and students alike. Traditionally, students would consume information provided by their teachers during direct instruction or by an analog textbook or reference materials, but this process has been positively disrupted by the advent of highly varied and interactive forms of digital media.

Teachers need no longer rely on a single textbook as the sole source of content information, because of the existence of so much digitally accessible content information and reference material. Students can now consume digitized, multisensory information when they are first interacting with or practicing and deepening new content knowledge. It is this multisensory aspect of digital media that adds more value by enhancing students' abilities to make connections between new information and their previously acquired background knowledge and experiences.

Nonetheless, the digital representation of media and information is not in and of itself transformational. Digitally represented media that are consumed by students and teachers reside in the translational use of technology—specifically in the consumption step of translational technologies. Consumption of rich, multisensory media certainly adds more value than the automation of mundane tasks. The level of interactivity varies among sources, but the nature of consuming digitally represented forms of knowledge is inherently multisensory, and consuming multimedia adds more value to the learning experience than consuming text in the absence of nonlinguistic representations (Magana & Marzano, 2014; Marzano, 2007; Mayer, 2001).

Again, it may be helpful to self-assess one's use of technology tools for consumption tasks. Use the questions in Table 3.3 to guide your own self-reflection on how you or your students typically use digital tools for the task of consuming content-related information and resources.

It should be noted that it was only a short time ago when the explosion of online resources enabled equitable access to a wide range of digital knowledge and information resources. This has significantly improved access to these

TABLE 3.3 ■ T1.2: Consumption—Guiding Questions for Translational Technology Use

Guiding Question	Response		Value Indicator
1. Do students use digital tools to consume content-related knowledge and information?	Yes	No	Access
2. Do students use digital tools to consume interactive content-related resources?	Yes	No	Access
3. Does student use of technology for information consumption result in time savings?	Yes	No	Efficiency

FRAMING TOOL T1.2
CONSUMPTION

1. What are the digital tools you use for the consumption of information or media?

   _____

   _____

   _____

   _____

2. What are the tasks to which you apply these tools?

   _____

   _____

   _____

   _____

3. How does the use of these tools add value?

   _____

   _____

   _____

   _____

4. What other tasks do you think might be enhanced by digital consumption tools?

   _____

   _____

   _____

   _____

Available for download at **www.corwin.com/disruptiveclassroomtech**

Copyright © 2017 by Corwin. All rights reserved. Reprinted from *Disruptive Classroom Technologies: A Framework for Innovation in Education* by Sonny Magana. Thousand Oaks, CA: Corwin, www.corwin.com. Reproduction authorized only for the local school site or nonprofit organization that has purchased this book.

resources for K–12 students. While there is still much work to do, school systems have done a great deal to bridge the digital divide and provide access to digital knowledge and information for our neediest learners. This adds value, but in terms of improving student learning performance and outcomes, using technology to access knowledge resources offers relatively low value compared with other types of technology use. Some of the digital resources that enable the digital consumption of media include the following:

- Digital textbooks
- E-books
- Digital newspapers and magazines
- Blogs, wikis, and podcasts
- Websites
- Compact discs
- DVDs
- Digital videos
- Digital music
- Digital slideshows
- Digital sound files
- Digital animations
- Digital multimedia presentations
- Digital games
- Smartphone apps

Again, it may be useful to unpack and reflect on the ways you think about and use technology tools to consume or have your students consume digital information or experiences. Answer the questions in Framing Tool T1.2 to help you think through how you use technology in your teaching, and once again, take notice of the pattern that emerges from your responses.

Once again, it may be useful to consider one's level of proficiency in regard to using technology to consume media and information. As consumption tasks naturally impact student learning, it may be helpful for educators to use a proficiency scale to categorize their use of educational technology for consumption tasks, as well as the impact of such tasks on student learning performance.

SUMMARY

Both stages of the T3 Framework discussed in this chapter—T1.1: Automation and T1.2: Consumption—represent translational uses of educational technology. They are necessary stages to go through, and while they add value in terms of automaticity, time saving, increasing efficiencies, and improving accuracy, they are insufficient in terms of transforming either the instructional or learning task itself, or the performer of the task. These types of educational technology tasks use digital tools to add value, but the value they add is relatively low.

Translational technology use does not substantively change the task, nor does it substantively change the person doing that task. If we expect to see a transformational impact from translational uses of technology, we are bound to be disappointed. This may be a reason for the underwhelming effect of educational technologies in general, as the predominant use of classroom technologies is translational in nature. One troubling aspect of this conundrum is that we keep misusing the terms *translational* and *transformational* or, even worse, using them interchangeably.

Doing the same thing over and over while expecting different results is an exercise in futility. Continuously engaging in translational uses of technology and expecting transformational results is, by at least one definition, insane. Yet that's what seems to be happening in educational systems the world over: teachers and students engaging in fundamentally translational technology uses and expecting transformational outcomes.

Only by reframing our experiences and reexamining our use of these terms will we free ourselves from the misapplication of these concepts, and that is the first step in unleashing the limitless potential of teachers and students to be more deliberately transformational in the way they use digital technology tools. So let's stop misapplying these terms and start applying the term *translational technology use* to situations such as the ones provided in this chapter. Reframing the translational use of technology is a necessary first step in helping educational systems think differently about realizing higher-value uses of technology in the service of teaching and learning. In the next chapter, we will explore transformational uses of educational technology.

4

T2: TRANSFORMATIONAL TECHNOLOGY USE

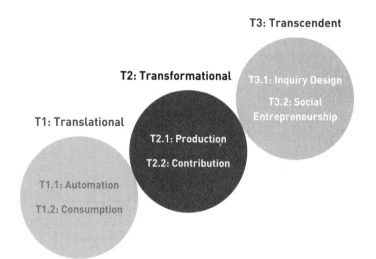

Once upon a time I dreamt I was a butterfly, fluttering hither and thither, enjoying itself to the full of its bent. Suddenly I awoke. Now I do not know whether it was then I dreamt I was a butterfly, or whether I am now a butterfly dreaming I am a man. Between a man and a butterfly there is necessarily a distinction. The transition is called the transformation of material things.

—Zhuangzi (c. 369–286 BCE)

TRANSFORMATIONAL TECHNOLOGY USE DEFINED

The origins of the word *transform* can be found in the Latin *transformare*: to make a thorough or dramatic change in substance, form, or character. It stands to reason that to be considered transformational, technology use must give rise to dramatic or substantive changes in both the task to which the technology tool is applied and the person enacting the task. To generate transformative value within an education context, the technology use ideally should (a) primarily focus on learners' achieving content and skill mastery and (b) catalyze a change in a learner's mindset, understanding, and cognizance to a higher-order state.

Albert Einstein once observed that the level of consciousness needed to generate a problem's solution must be of a higher order than that which created the problem. In the context of learning, an arguable implication of this observation is that the construction of deep conceptual understanding through rigorous problem solving enacts substantive changes in a learner's consciousness. Between the novice and the master, there is a necessary distinction. This transition engenders a cognitive transformation from a novice state of consciousness to a higher-level state of mastery. For example, when students struggle to master some challenging new knowledge or skill, say in algebra, biology, calculus, or physics, their cognitive capacity is clearly changed. They no longer think of the problems they first encountered in quite the same way. Perhaps more important, students also discover something new about themselves through the process of mindfully investing effort to master new knowledge or skills, and they begin the happy process of recognizing and strengthening the direct causal relationship between effort and achievement. Successful growth-focused learning experiences tend to increase students' confidence, agency, and willingness to take intellectual risks beyond the known limits of their cognitive comfort zones (Dweck, 2006).

Learning for mastery might also be considered an iterative process of achieving wisdom through continuously accumulating knowledge and meaningful experience. This reflects what the great educator and humanitarian Paolo Freire (1973) referred to as educational emancipation; each time students are liberated from the oppressive forces of cognitive misconceptions, misapprehension, and self-doubt, they ascend toward higher states of consciousness while their nascent limitless learning potential becomes that much more fully realized. Perhaps this can best be illustrated through the concept of accretion: When a grain of sand gets trapped inside an oyster's body, the organism tries to ease its discomfort by surrounding the irritant with layer upon layer of calcium carbonate, which ultimately coalesces into a pearl; when learners struggle through the discomfort associated with transformational growth, not only are they transformed from novices to masters, but over time their combined and applied understanding and experiences crystalize into pearls of wisdom.

In the context of learning systems, there appears to be no common definition or interpretation of transformation with technology, nor is there much agreement on exactly what is being transformed. In the context of the T3 Framework, I'd like to offer a definition of transformational technology use in education: the intentional application of digital technologies to unleash students' learning expertise, in ways not possible without technology, to achieve ever higher levels of knowledge and mastery. This definition puts at the center of the transformational experience technology's potential impact on unleashing students' unlimited learning capacity.

In the context of my teaching career, I have had a number of transformational experiences with educational technology. One such watershed moment forever changed the way I thought about the uses of technologies in service of teaching and learning. In the summer of 1991, I was awarded a modest grant, purchased a 300 baud modem, and connected my classroom to the recently declassified Internet. One of the components of the grant was to capture qualitative data regarding teachers' experiences in an action research project aimed at ascertaining the potential impact of the Internet on student engagement and achievement (Magana, Lovejoy, Nafissian, & Reynaud, 1993).

> Transformational technology use in education: the intentional application of digital technologies to unleash students' learning expertise, in ways not possible without technology, to achieve ever higher levels of knowledge and mastery.

I joined a virtual community of teachers and students called the International Education and Resource Network (iEARN). At its inception a few years earlier, iEARN established its mission to build mutual respect and understanding by engaging students in global collaborative online projects that empowered youth to both address and produce resolutions for problems facing humanity and the planet.

One of the iEARN projects that piqued my curiosity was the US–Soviet Exchange Project, developed to establish the first-ever digital dialogue between students in American and Soviet schools. The objective of the US–Soviet Exchange Project was to establish and build relationships between citizens of the United States and the Soviet Union through this new form of communication that was called electronic mail, or e-mail.

Mikhail Gorbachev, then the president of the Soviet Union, had recently established policies promoting *glasnost,* the open exchange of knowledge, information, and culture between the East and the West as a means of transforming Cold War animosity. Gorbachev had overseen the creation of GlasNet, the early Soviet Internet and e-mail platform, which was made available to research institutions, universities—and public schools. For the first time in history, teachers and students in public schools in the Soviet Union could begin to build a digital dialogue with the Western world, bridging geographic, cultural, and political boundaries using electronic communications.

Then on August 19, 1991, a remarkable thing happened: Hard-line members of the Communist Party of the Soviet Union, enraged by Gorbachev's reforms, enacted a coup d'état and kidnapped Gorbachev and his wife, Raisa. This military junta enacted a type of Soviet-style martial law in Moscow, ratcheting up the uncertainty and fears in Soviet citizens and the world at large. This was most alarming in light of the recent progress made between the United States and the Soviet Union; political discourse was established between Presidents Reagan and Gorbachev, as were tenuous diplomatic relations. This new turn of events could potentially plunge the Soviet Union back into Cold War–era communist control and increased animosity, and possible aggression, toward the West.

The coup leaders hamstrung the world press, effectively severing radio and television news feeds from Moscow to the rest of the world. Fearing a return to the Communist tactics emblematic of the Cold War, the world outside waited anxiously for news from behind the newly drawn Iron Curtain. But there was one information feed the coup leaders did not consider: the Internet.

While the rest of the world waited for news from Moscow, I was in regular e-mail communication through iEARN with teachers in Moscow, who shared their personal stories and observations with me. They described the intimidating Soviet military presence in their home—tanks rumbling through the streets and soldiers in armored vehicles patrolling Moscow neighborhoods, quelling any potential unrest. Through e-mail, my new friends expressed the very real dread they felt that their country was slipping back toward Cold War–era breadlines, oppression, and pervasive fear. Many expressed their support for an uprising protest and calls for participating in a civil strike across the Soviet capital.

Almost as quickly as it started, the coup was over and Gorbachev was returned to power. For the next several months, through e-mail exchanges as part of the US–Soviet Exchange Project, my students and I witnessed the final dissolution of the Soviet Union and the emergence of modern Russia. My students and our partner students in Moscow schools contributed to each other's understanding of our respective cultures, collaboratively producing and exchanging numerous learning artifacts such as newsletter articles, surveys, short stories, essays, poetry, and films. Our fear of citizens living in the "evil empire," as President Reagan referred to the Soviet Union, was transformed into mutual respect and deeper understanding of our Soviet partners. This transition was clearly reflected in the knowledge products our students created. Through this project, we realized how common were the hopes and dreams of students living in the transforming Russian Federation and my students here in the United States. They wanted to pursue life, freedom, and happiness just as we did. Moreover, my students and I realized that we were not only witnessing history but were participants in historic events made possible through a historic medium—global e-mail.

Participation in the US–Soviet Exchange Project was a transformational experience. Not only did the technology use allow us to do new things in new ways, but it enabled us to create and digitize our thought products, which, through the collaborative production and contribution of these artifacts, helped us understand that our separateness from the Soviets was an illusion. We awakened from a decades-long, nightmarish threat of US–Soviet nuclear annihilation to a new, higher level of consciousness regarding our new friends from the Soviet Union. Our mindsets had shifted. We had become valued, contributive members of a global citizenry.

This experience of using new technology in a transformational way forever changed me as a teacher and educational technologist. It clearly would not have been possible for my students and me to have such immediate, relevant, and profound experiences with our Soviet partners without global e-mail technology. That is what led me to begin posing the following question addressing how technology adds value to teaching and learning: "How can students use technology to represent what they know, what they are able to do, and how they think, in ways that are not possible without the technology?" That question helped me frame innovative uses of educational technologies in my classroom for many years to come. Moreover, this question can be applied to just about any learning context, content area, or grade level. For example, any teacher, or student, can readily apply this question as it relates to students' use of technology to generate a variety of means of representing their understanding of and thinking about key concepts in mathematics, English language arts, science, history, or any other content area.

A critical shift that is indicative of the transformational use of technology in classrooms is transferring the locus of control of the learning experience, and the cognitive load, from teachers to students. When this shift happens, students begin using technologies to express to themselves and others their understanding of new content knowledge. Capturing their learning in the form of student-generated, digital knowledge products allows students to learn from the process of representing their learning in multiple ways. These knowledge products can be any type of authentically produced student-generated evidence of their learning. There are no known limits to what these products might look like (Magana & Marzano, 2014). This is a process of active learning reflection that creates iterations of digital artifacts that represent what students know and are able to do and, more important, how they think about what they know and are able to do.

The two steps in the transformational stage of educational technologies are T2.1: Production and T2.2: Contribution. Both of these levels reflect the way technology can be used by students to positively disrupt translational technology use and enact transformational technology use—the Chuck Berry phase of technology use. The two steps of transformational technology use in education—production and contribution—will be described in the next sections.

T2.1: PRODUCTION

In the late 20th century, futurist Alvin Toffler (1970) predicted that the roles of producers and consumers would begin to blur, merging into a new hybrid individual. Toffler (1970) coined the term *prosumer* to describe a person who, empowered by disruptive technologies, would be able to both produce and consume media. The digital revolution, particularly the advent of Web 2.0 and "maker" technologies, enabled a kind of mass availability of production technologies, which hastened the evolution of the prosumer on a scale never before seen.

The prosumer revolution has given rise to a generation of students who produce as much—if not more—media and content as they consume. Today's students are compelled by their binary birthright to produce digital representations of their knowledge—or digital knowledge artifacts—that can be archived, can be accessed, and will remain free from degradation; for unlike their analog counterparts, such as photographs, drawings, texts, paintings, and so on, digital artifacts are composed of 1s and 0s, which do not degrade over time.

It's important to broaden the definition of production in this context to include three critical elements: (1) student production of authentic evidence of growth and mastery using digital tools, (2) the quality of knowledge artifacts that students produce with digital tools, and (3) the "thought pathways" students have followed to create those artifacts. In terms of metacognitive value for the student and teacher alike, making students' thinking processes explicit is perhaps even more important than the production of objects that represent their thinking.

There are three student production strategies associated with T2.1: Production. Student use of technology to these ends satisfies the definition of transformative technology use, as both the task of representing knowledge by constructing digital artifacts and the task of making explicit the thinking that underpins these products engenders substantive changes in these learning tasks and the students enacting them. Instead of simply translating tasks and experiences from an analog to a digital modality, students use technology not only to experience new knowledge but to apply that knowledge in the production of an authentic digital artifact that represents what students know and how they came to know it.

> Students use technology not only to experience new knowledge but to apply that knowledge in the production of an authentic digital artifact that represents what students know and how they came to know it.

Once again, it might be helpful to consider the extent to which students' technology use represents the production stage by posing some guiding questions. Some questions that may help you think about and evaluate how you implement the production stage of technology use are listed in Table 4.1. These strategies are discussed in more detail in the following sections.

TABLE 4.1 ■ T2.1: Production—Guiding Questions for Transformational Technology Use		
Guiding Question	**Response**	**Value Indicator**
1. Do students use digital technologies to produce, review, archive, and update personal mastery goals?	Yes No	Creating and communicating mastery goals
2. Do students use digital technologies to continuously track and visualize their growth toward their mastery goals?	Yes No	Monitoring and visualizing growth
3. Do students use technology tools to produce, archive, and review authentic knowledge artifacts that represent what students know and are able to do while making their thinking explicit?	Yes No	Multiple means of representing knowledge and thinking

T2.1-1: Students Produce Personal Mastery Goals

A reasonable starting point for student production with technology resides within the key concepts addressed by content learning standards. These key concepts represent the essential knowledge that students need to acquire in core content areas. These concepts are represented by either national or other comprehensive state learning standards (e.g., the state learning standards from Texas, Florida, or Virginia) or Advanced Placement or International Baccalaureate standards. Think of key concepts as the critical knowledge and skills we desire students to master.

Having teachers communicate clear learning goals to their students and then monitor student progress with some proficiency scale is associated with moderate to large effect sizes (Hattie, 2009; Haystead & Marzano, 2010; Marzano, 2007). This is significant, and teachers would be well served to continue applying and expanding on this practice. However, engaging students in the discipline of developing their own goals and then regularly tracking their progress and the effort they expend toward achieving those goals is associated with a very large effect size—the equivalent of a 32-percentile-point gain in student achievement (Haystead & Marzano, 2009b). Moreover, asking students to express connections between their unique personal attributes that affirm a sense of adequacy and their capacity to set and realize important goals not only heightens students' sense of self-efficacy but is associated with a 40% increase in student academic achievement (Meyer, Rose, & Gordon, 2014).

Giving students the opportunity to establish meaningful goals and then keep track of their progress and the effort they expend toward realizing those goals transforms their role from passive followers of extrinsic goals to active developers and enactors of intrinsic goals (Magana & Marzano, 2014). In terms of transformational technology use, having students use digital tools to enhance this process is rather low-hanging fruit: It is easy to do, engenders very little risk, and has a substantial upside. Consider having students use digital tools to engage in the following tasks:

1. Produce personal mastery goals that represent their own unique talents, skills, competencies, and attributes

2. Produce a simple proficiency scale to help them mindfully monitor their progress toward their mastery goals

3. Keep track of their progress and effort they invest toward achieving their mastery goals

Simply defined, a learning goal is a statement that represents the knowledge students will gain as a result of the instruction they receive and activities they do in a given content lesson. New knowledge that students gain and are able to declare is referred to as *declarative knowledge,* while knowledge that represents some new skill, strategy, or procedure is known as *procedural knowledge.* For example, a common learning goal format for declarative and procedural knowledge may be as follows: Students will understand _____, (declare their knowledge gain) and be able to _____ (demonstrate a new skill, strategy, or procedure) (Magana & Marzano, 2014, 2015; Marzano, 2007).

However, these tasks and the cognitive load associated with them are typically borne by teachers, not students. Shifting to the students the tasks of producing and representing goals, monitoring progress with proficiency scales, and producing with digital tools assessment artifacts representing knowledge gain is reflective of transformational uses of technology.

Student mastery goals differ from traditional learning goals in that they are generated by students and are specific, strategic, and measurable. Specific mastery goals can be far more effective than goals that are imprecise and therefore open to equivocation or misinterpretation. Mastery goals that are specific generally address a unidimensional skill rather than a complex, multidimensional learning standard that may have three or more dimensions of learning. Moreover, mastery goals that are strategic prompt students to think about the tasks they need to implement to achieve their goals and evoke executive or strategic functioning of the neocortex (Meyer et al., 2014). Finally, mastery goals that are measurable through the use of an incremental scale are more likely to reduce the ambiguity associated with how learners may specifically improve their performance (Roessger, 2016).

It may be helpful to provide students with sentence stems to prompt their production of mastery goals. A sample mastery goal sentence stem might be as follows:

SPECIFIC: I will master _____ by _____.
                                (Goal or skill)   (Date)

STRATEGIC: To achieve mastery, I will need to _____.
                                             (Actions)

MEASURABLE: I will track my progress _____ by _____.
                                    (Frequency)   (Actions)

A completed student mastery goal sentence may look like the following:

SPECIFIC: I will master <u>place value within 1,000,000</u> by <u>September 30</u>.
                                (Goal or skill)   (Date)

STRATEGIC: To achieve mastery, I will need to <u>solve place value problems every day for 15 minutes until I don't make *any* errors</u>.
                                           (Actions)

MEASURABLE: I will track my progress <u>weekly</u> by <u>checking with my teacher</u>.
                                  (Frequency)   (Actions)

These sentence-stem examples may be of benefit to students initially. However, once students get into the discipline of creating mastery goals, deciding what plan they need to follow to achieve those goals, and measuring their progress toward their goals, they will begin to create far more varied and creative strategies and metrics. Give students ample opportunities to engage in cumulative reviews of their mastery goals to engage in continuous reflection on their knowledge growth over time. This will help students become more mindful, self-regulating, and deeply reflective experts on *how they themselves learn best*.

Some useful digital resources that can enable the production of mastery goals and tracking progress are listed in Table 4.2.

T2.1-2: Students Track and Visualize Their Growth and Mastery

While it's important for teachers to track student progress, it is even more important for students to produce, reflect on, and track their own progress toward mastery (Magana & Marzano, 2014; Marzano, 2007). Giving students the opportunity to set mastery learning goals and regularly track their growth is inherently

TABLE 4.2 ■ Educational Technologies for Producing Mastery Goals			
Task	**Digital Tools**	**User**	**Tool Category**
Creating and archiving mastery goals	Evernote Google Drive Microsoft Office 365 Microsoft OneNote Padlet Promethean's ClassFlow	Students	Cloud-based, open-ended, multimedia productivity tools

motivating for students. Enhancing this process with graphic, or nonlinguistic, representations of their growth will help students "see" their progress and can help enhance students' active self-reflection and self-regulation (Magana & Marzano, 2014; Marzano, 2007). Over time, the discipline of setting mastery goals, investing energy to achieve those goals, and monitoring their progress toward their goals will not only help build students' self-awareness but will also unleash their potential for self-determination.

It would be helpful for students to quantify their levels of knowledge gain using a simple numerical proficiency scale. Producing and monitoring their progress using a simple proficiency scale will help students represent with greater precision what they understand and what they aim to understand (Magana & Marzano, 2014; Marzano, 2007). An effective way to do this is to create a three-point scale that includes incremental indicators of student growth. A sample student mastery scale is shown in Table 4.3.

It's important to modify the language of the proficiency scale so the indicators reflect students' vocabulary and understanding. Even better, have students develop

TABLE 4.3 ■ Sample Proficiency Scale for Student Mastery Goals	
Proficiency Score	**Indicator**
3	**Mastery:** Students demonstrate, model, and communicate conceptual understanding of content that is free from critical errors or oversights.
2	**Nearing mastery:** Students are beginning to demonstrate, model, and communicate some conceptual understanding of content, but with critical errors or oversights.
1	**Not near mastery:** Students have not yet demonstrated, modeled, or communicated conceptual understanding.

the language that is used in the indicators of growth. This will help ensure student ownership of both the assessment and learning process (Magana & Marzano, 2014). Consider using the Student Progress and Effort Tracker template that was built using a Google spreadsheet (see Figure 4.1 on the next page). The template can be downloaded through this link: https://goo.gl/91fst6.

> Giving students the opportunity to set mastery learning goals and regularly track their growth is inherently motivating for students.

Some useful digital resources that can enable the production of mastery goals and tracking progress are listed in Table 4.4.

TABLE 4.4 ■ Educational Technologies for Tracking Mastery Goals

Task	Digital Tools	Cost	Tool Category
Crafting, communicating, tracking, and archiving mastery goals	Google Drive (Google spreadsheet) Microsoft Office 365 Microsoft OneNote	0 0 0 0	Open-ended, multimedia productivity tools
Monitoring student progress toward mastery goals	MasterTrack (MasterTrackSolutions.com)	$	Cloud-based student mastery tracking tool

T2.1-3: Students Produce and Archive Authentic Knowledge and Thought Artifacts

The third production strategy involves students' using digital tools to create authentic multimedia representations of their declarative and procedural knowledge and to make their thinking regarding both explicit. Shifting the tasks of producing authentic formative assessment representations from teachers to students is illustrative of transformational technology use, because this allows students the opportunities to become the designers of multiple means of representing what they know, what they are able to do, and how they think about what they know and are able to do (Meyer et al., 2014).

Much has come to light about the benefits of formative assessment as a process (Marzano, 2007). While summative assessments are used to measure student knowledge gained from instruction, formative assessments are used to ascertain student knowledge gained during instruction. Formative assessments can take many forms, but they are typically generated by teachers. A powerful category of formative assessments includes those that are generated by students.

FIGURE 4.1 ■ Student Progress and Effort Tracker Template

Student	Teacher	Class	Date Started	Date Ended
Joey Ramone	Miss Gradenko	Math	1-Sep	30-Sep

Mastery Goal: I will master place value to 1,000,000 by September 30.

What I'll Do to Achieve Mastery: I will practice this skill for 20 minutes each day, I will reflect on my progress and effort at least once weekly, and I will check in with my teacher every week to share my progress and effort.

	1 Not Yet Mastering	2 Nearing Mastery	3 Mastering
Progress Scale	I have not yet demonstrated, modeled, or communicated my full understanding.	I am beginning to demonstrate, model, and communicate some understanding but still have some errors.	I can demonstrate, model, and communicate full understanding without errors or oversights.
	1 Not Yet Full Effort	2 Nearing Full Effort	3 Full Effort
Effort Scale	I have not yet put my full effort to learn this skill yet.	I am beginning to put my full effort to learn this skill.	I am putting my full effort to learn this skill to the best of my ability.

Date	Progress	Effort	Reflections
1-Sep	1	1	I'm not able to demonstrate this skill. I feel frustrated. :-(
8-Sep	1.5	1	YIKES! It is going to take a lot more work to understand this! :-(
15-Sep	2	2.5	I think I'm starting to understand but still have to work harder. :-/
22-Sep	2	2.5	I am really working hard but keep making the same mistakes. :-/
29-Sep	2.5	3	I am understanding more and am making fewer mistakes! :-)
30-Sep	3	3	YAY!! I have mastered this skill and am ready for the next one! :-) :-)

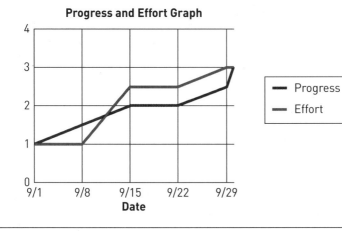

Progress and Effort Graph

Note: Template available at https://goo.gl/91fst6

These types of assessments are referred to as student-generated assessments (Magana & Marzano, 2014). Student-generated assessments originate from within students' own sets of cognitive constructs and can take multiple forms. When students are given the opportunity to generate multiple ways of representing their knowledge, they start taking ownership for the process of representing what they know and are able to do and how they think about their learning (Magana & Marzano, 2015).

The most common form of student-generated assessment is individual conversations between students and teachers in which the student verbally expresses his or her understanding of content knowledge. Rather than simply choosing one right answer out of a predetermined series of choices or providing a short constructed response, the learners are crafting, sharing, and defending a deeply informative narrative about their learning. Talking about their knowledge gains allows students to engage in reflection "on the spot" as they express the thinking journey that underpins their particular knowledge representations. Students make explicit their thinking about their knowledge through assessment conversations using their own words, elaborations, analogies, and evidence. This allows teachers to ascertain both the quality and the correctness of students' thinking processes as made explicit through the student narratives. This is a far more informative, and therefore valuable, way of assessing authentic student knowledge gain (Magana & Marzano, 2015).

Teachers who are assessing student growth and learning may also pose probing questions to the students, asking for clarifications, elaborations, or further evidence to support the students' particular ways of expressing knowledge and thought, in a manner that is both personalized and responsive to the learner. As the learner is directly responsible for making decisions about the way his or her knowledge gain is expressed, one can readily see why this highly personalized form of assessment can be so powerful. One can also see why this process is so rarely used: It takes much more time than is typically available to classroom teachers.

The constraint of limited time provides an opportunity to integrate digital productivity technologies to disrupt the ways teachers authentically assess student knowledge and growth. Have students use a range of digital recording tools to produce, capture, and archive knowledge artifacts representing knowledge gain and thought pathways. With readily available cloud-based production technologies, teachers can transform their classrooms from models of knowledge transmission—where knowledge is transmitted from the teacher to the student—to models of knowledge production in which students generate knowledge products that make their thinking explicit.

The notion of making student thinking visible, while certainly a breakthrough in learning philosophy, implies a particular visual bias and perhaps even a limitation on representational forms of thinking (Ritchhart, Church, & Morrison, 2011). Rather, the concept of making thinking explicit offers limitless pathways for students to exhibit their thinking by incorporating digital tools to create multisensory expressions of authentic knowledge and thought. These may include but are not limited to sound, movement, images, videos, the spoken word, oral narrations embedded in text, music, poetry, song lyrics, or any digital file that includes, rather than excludes, a wide variety of media. Multimedia artifacts created by learners become de facto thought products that can be digitally archived and accessed.

This idea requires a disruption in the way we typically think about assessing student knowledge gain—specifically, using only teacher-generated assessments. For example, consider offering students multiple options for representing their knowledge gain and their thinking—one of the hallmark strategies in the Universal Design for Learning framework (Meyer et al., 2014). Have students use free digital tools such as Audacity to record an oral representation of what they know, what they are able to do, and how they think about their learning. Or have students use multimedia tools such as VoiceThread to record a layer of narration over a PowerPoint presentation, word-processing document, or image file. Students can also use a variety of screencast tools such as Jing, Screencast-O-Matic, or Screencastify to record annotations and narration on any file that appears on their computer screen (Magana & Marzano, 2015). Or have students use free open-ended multimedia production suites such as Microsoft OneNote or Promethean's ClassFlow to generate student-centered evidence of their learning while making their thinking explicit using a multiplicity of media. There are no limits to how students might creatively use these tools to represent their learning.

> Making thinking explicit offers limitless pathways for students to exhibit their thinking by incorporating digital tools to create multisensory expressions of authentic knowledge and thought.

Students can use many of the tools mentioned in the translational section to produce, archive, and share knowledge artifacts with their teachers. Cloud-based word-processing, presentation, and spreadsheet tools can all be used in the production stage, as students can readily use these technology tools to produce knowledge artifacts that represent their growth and how they think about the academic content.

In addition to open-ended productivity tools, another category of useful educational technology is screencast tools. Screencast tools record from full- or modified-screen videos that capture anything displayed on the computer screen, along with an accompanying audio track. The unique screen and audio-recording capability of screencast tools allows students to use a wide variety of digital multimedia tools to produce representations of their knowledge while capturing auditory narration to coincide with their presentations. Students can use screencast tools to record their annotations, presentations, or any other digital representation of their learning using desktop computers, laptops, tablets, iPads, or even smartphones. Once completed, students' screencast videos can be archived using a variety of hosting sites. A list of readily available production/screencast recording tools and archiving tools is shown in Table 4.5. All these tools are relatively easy to learn, and most are free; others offer optional premium upgrades to feature-laden versions.

Again, it may be useful to unpack the ways you think about and use digital tools to have students engage in the process of production—specifically,

TABLE 4.5 ■ Educational Technologies for Producing Knowledge and Thought Artifacts				
Task	Digital Production/ Screencast Tools	Cost	Digital Archiving Tools	Cost
Students creating, archiving, and reviewing authentic knowledge and thinking artifacts	Adobe Presenter	$$	YouTube	0
	Adobe Spark	0	TeacherTube	0
	Camtasia Studio	$$$	Vimeo	0
	Doceri	0–$	Screencast.com	0–$
	EduCreations	0	Acclaim	0
	ExplainEverything	$	Google Sites	0
	Google Docs	0		
	Google Presentation	0		
	Google	0–$		
	Google Apps	0		
	Haiku Deck	0–$		
	Knowmia	0		
	Microsoft Office Mix	0–$		
	Microsoft OneNote	0		
	PowToon	0		
	Screencastify	0		
	Screencast-O-Matic	$		
	ScreenChomp	0		
	ClassFlow	0–$		
	ShowMe	0		
	ThingLink	0		
	TouchCast	0		
	VoiceThread	0		

FRAMING TOOL T2.1
PRODUCTION

1. What are the digital tools that your students use for production?

   _____

   _____

   _____

   _____

2. What are the tasks to which students apply those tools?

   _____

   _____

   _____

   _____

3. How does the use of those tools add value?

   _____

   _____

   _____

   _____

4. What other student production tasks do you think might be enhanced by digital production tools?

   _____

   _____

   _____

   _____

Available for download at **www.corwin.com/disruptiveclassroomtech**

Copyright © 2017 by Corwin. All rights reserved. Reprinted from *Disruptive Classroom Technologies: A Framework for Innovation in Education* by Sonny Magana. Thousand Oaks, CA: Corwin, www.corwin.com. Reproduction authorized only for the local school site or nonprofit organization that has purchased this book.

producing mastery learning goals that can be tracked and visualized and producing authentic knowledge artifacts that represent growth in student knowledge and thought. This is part of the process of reflecting on the "here and now" of your practices with technology and the available resources in your classroom or school. Answer the questions in Framing Tool T2.1 to help you think about how you use technology in your teaching, and be sure to notice the picture that emerges.

T2.2: CONTRIBUTION

The second stage in the area of transformative technology use in education is contribution—a stage that incorporates all three previous levels in the framework. Contribution is the incremental stage in which students use technology to produce and exhibit digital artifacts that will contribute not only to their own knowledge but to the knowledge of others as well. To achieve this stage, teachers and students will need to have developed interdependent learning environments that function more like learning communities than competitive arenas. Students learn better collectively than in isolation, and classrooms that are more conducive to contribution tend to support the growth of the whole group. In such contributive classrooms, students mindfully wield educational technology tools to automate routine tasks, consume and scrutinize a wide variety of information from digital sources, and then synthesize their understanding by producing artifacts of their knowledge and thinking journeys; however, to reach the contribution stage, students need to engage in the task of intentionally designing and creating knowledge products with the express purpose of contributing their unique perspectives and interpretations to the knowledge gains of others.

Most teachers will likely agree that we learn the most about any content when we work to elicit understanding about that content from students—particularly students with limited background knowledge about the content we are teaching. Giving students the opportunity to use digital tools to teach others what they know, what they are able to do, and how they think about their knowledge is fundamentally transformational, because the students' role is substantively changed from that of student to teacher.

> Giving students the opportunity to use digital tools to teach others what they know, what they are able to do, and how they think about their knowledge is fundamentally transformational, because the students' role is substantively changed from that of student to teacher.

Moreover, it's important to give students opportunities to learn how to step outside of their own way of thinking and put themselves in another person's frame of mind. Students learn how to empathize with the "end user" when engaging in the design and production of knowledge resources that aid another person's learning journey. This gives students the opportunity to develop empathy and consideration for the way others interpret and experience new information and knowledge. The notion of student contribution, while not new, can only enhance the important role of student cooperation and collaboration, perhaps to an even higher degree.

Use the questions in Table 4.6 to guide your self-reflection and self-assessment of how your students use digital tools for contribution tasks.

TABLE 4.6 ■ T2.2: Contribution—Guiding Questions for Transformational Technology Use

Guiding Question	Response		Value Indicator
1. Do students use digital tools to contribute to and track their observance of classroom promises and commitments?	Yes	No	Contribution to the classroom environment
2. Do students use digital tools to produce authentic tutorials designed to contribute to others' learning?	Yes	No	Contribution to the learning community
3. Do students use digital tools to curate their authentic learning tutorials?	Yes	No	Contribution to the learning community

Each of these questions is underpinned by strategies that can be used immediately to improve the level of contribution in classrooms. An exploration of each strategy follows.

T2.2-1: Students Contribute to and Track Their Observance of Classroom Promises and Commitments

All effective classrooms have well-established and observed rules and procedures. This is a critical element of effective instructional practice (Marzano, 2007). However, most classroom rules and procedures are developed without significant input or contribution from the very people who, we hope, will adhere to those rules and procedures. This begs the question of ownership related to those rules and procedures. Students who have substantive input into the norms and expectations for the learning environment are more likely to act in accordance with those expectations, because they have had some stake in their development and therefore have a greater degree of ownership over them (Magana & Marzano, 2014).

Giving students the opportunity to contribute to the development of the norms and expectations of the classroom is highly democratic, inclusive, and contributive. However, rules and expectations are extrinsic; they typically derive from outside one's self. On the other hand, promises and commitments are more intrinsic; they emanate from within. A promise or a commitment is something that is quite natural for us to "own."

Moreover, group promises or commitments are owned collectively. That is why I suggest shifting the language of classroom rules and expectations toward use of the terms *promises* and *commitments*. On the first day of class, ask your students to work in groups to come up with the conditions that are most conducive to how they learn best. Working in contributive groups, have students brainstorm, compile, and discuss potential classroom promises and commitments using a variety of technology tools, such as those shown in Table 4.5. Some prompting may be necessary, so consider scaffolding this process for students with some promises and commitments that you will make as the teacher.

Model democratic interaction in your classroom by having students use free voting tools to reach consensus on the promises and commitments of their classroom. Depending on the ages of your students, you can generate a classroom contract that reflects the promises and commitments, or have students do so using any of the tools listed in Table 4.7. Finally, consider using a free online behavior tracking tool such as ClassDojo to celebrate students when they exhibit behaviors and decisions that reflect the classroom promises and commitments. A list of digital tools that can be used to empower students to contribute to and monitor observance of classroom promises and commitments is shown in Table 4.7.

TABLE 4.7 ■ Technologies for Creating and Monitoring Classroom Promises and Commitments

Task	Digital Tools	Cost
Students brainstorming, creating, and communicating classroom promises and commitments	Google Drive	0
	Microsoft Office	0
	Mix	0
	Microsoft OneNote	0
Students voting and generating consensus for classroom promises and commitments	Google Drive	0
	(Google Forms)	0
	MicroPoll	0
	Plickers	0
	PollDaddy	0–$$$
	PollEverywhere	0–$$$
	Socrative	0–$
Monitoring student observance of classroom promises and commitments	ClassDojo	0

T2.2-2: Students Produce Authentic Tutorials
Designed to Contribute to Others' Learning

Too many students are relegated to passive, consumptive roles in today's class-rooms. With digital tools, it is now not only possible but also relatively easy to have students create multimedia tutorials, not just to make their thinking explicit to their teachers but to teach what they know to someone else. This changes the very nature of the task of creating multimedia knowledge products. This is a fundamentally transformative experience.

An inverse relationship exists between content-area expertise and empathy for novice misconceptions (Mazur, 2009). The more we know about a subject, the less likely we are to apprehend someone's making what to us are "simple" mistakes. This gives rise to a form of "expert bias" and can undermine efforts to effectively elicit understanding from others. Novice learners, on the other hand, lack this bias and are wonderfully positioned to explain how they identified, clarified, and rectified errors in their thinking.

Using the screencast and multimedia authoring tools shown in Table 4.5, students can produce digital knowledge products that not only make their thinking explicit but contribute to each other's learning. Students can wield such tools to find their unique "teaching voice," which they can use to teach someone else the unique ways they go about constructing knowledge, understanding, and meaning from academic content. These artifacts can also become a window into children's self-system views: how they think about the content, themselves, and the context in which they are representing new knowledge. Such learning categorizes highly engaging and empowering epistemic experiences.

When students produce and share learning tutorials within and between classrooms in a school, the level of contribution and sense of community will increase. The level of contribution is the ultimate level of educational transformation, as this gives learners the opportunity to represent and share knowledge they now know or understand. This substantively shifts students' roles from passive consumers of information and media to active developers of learning products that are designed to contribute to the community knowledge base. Changing the role of students from passive information consumers to active knowledge producers and contributors to others' knowledge represents, by its very nature, high-value transformational use of technology.

Imagine one classroom sourcing the learning resources that are used by students in that classroom. Now imagine every classroom in a school creating tutorials that can be used schoolwide. I call this idea "class-sourcing." Much like companies that use crowdsourcing to distribute tasks to anyone with a device and an Internet connection, teachers can tap into students' contributive nature to class-source learning resources that support and celebrate the growth of everyone in the classroom or school learning community and beyond.

This is a highly scalable notion. It ties into our innate desire to become valued and contributing members of some social cohort (Dreikurs, 1964). This drive has allowed humans to evolve, adapt, and survive. We are social animals, and our complex social structures and collective activities are precisely why we have survived—and even thrived—in hostile environments while other, less contribution-oriented species have not. Class-sourcing affords students authentic opportunities to learn and contribute their knowledge at very young ages, making it more likely that they will continue doing so for a lifetime of contribution to the sum total of human knowledge. This is where the use of educational technology adds the highest possible value in terms of the students' construction of knowledge products and the dissemination of those products to a large, authentic audience. This is really about kids having authentic reasons to engage in authentic learning tasks for authentic audiences.

Contribution is an idea whose time has come in public education. It's time for whole learning systems to engage in contributive learning practices that are designed to help everyone learn to the fullest extent while also helping everyone experience the joy of unleashing the limitless potential of every learner. This is not a radical idea. This is the essence of teamwork.

T2.2-3: Students Use Digital Tools to Curate Their Authentic Learning Tutorials

Previous generations of learners typically kept scrapbooks filled with reports, writing samples, photographs, or other learning artifacts tucked away in dusty boxes. These types of analog knowledge products, while valuable, are neither readily accessible nor extensible and are therefore not as useful as a platform for prompting continuous mastery learning. Using free cloud-based hosting technologies, learners can now readily archive and access digital "process-folios" containing iterative multimedia knowledge products created over the course of their lifetimes. By constantly reviewing those products, students establish and realize their own personal goals for achieving mastery.

Students today can create and curate authentic online "learning museums," complete with exhibits cataloguing their digital knowledge products. This process of reviewing their knowledge products will prompt students to naturally engage in reflection, metacognition, and knowledge revision by comparing the similarities and differences between older and newer exhibits of their knowledge. By deliberately conducting error analyses of their knowledge exhibitions, learners can continually update and revise their knowledge products and through the process of iteration generate entirely new ways of representing what they know and are able to do. Moreover, students can share, reflect on, and comment on each other's digital tutorials, making elaborations of new learning pathways explicit to themselves and others.

Imagine a class where every student is fully invested in the success of every other student—both socially and academically. This reflects the concept of interdependent contingency: the development of a classroom where every individual recognizes his or her own interdependence and connectedness to everyone else in the classroom system (Magana & Marzano, 2014; Marzano, 2007). It's entirely reasonable to develop a contributive mindset in classrooms by raising student contribution to the learning community as the paramount value. This process can be enhanced and scaled by having students regularly use educational technology tools for contribution. Having students wield technology tools to elicit, enhance, and support understanding from the entire class results in a much higher value added by technology. This leads to the issue of storing and managing all the digital contributive learning assets produced by students in your classroom.

Several years ago I met a remarkable teacher who embodies a contributive mindset. Eric Marcos teaches in Santa Monica, California. Along with his middle school students, Eric created an exemplary contributive website, www.mathtrain.tv. Eric and his students at Lincoln Middle School created this blog to capture all the knowledge tutorials that students created using screencast tools. But mathtrain.tv goes further than just having this group of students teach Mr. Marcos and one another what they know about math; these students have created tutorials with the specific objective of teaching the math concepts that they have actualized to middle school students anywhere on the planet. Eric has transformed his classroom learning environment into a globally contributive working space. The students in his class are not only contributing locally but sharing their tutorials globally; to date, viewers from around the world have watched math tutorials created by Eric's students more than 1.6 million times. They are making a powerful contribution to math students around the world.

This is a wonderful example that can be replicated with readily available production tools that are wielded in a contributive fashion. This will transform classrooms from competitive to more contributive learning spaces. It can't be overstated that any teacher can do this, regardless of grade level or content area. Anyone can take Eric's inspirational example and apply the ideals of contribution with technology in their classroom environment, using the digital tools mentioned earlier in this chapter. Shifting the tasks of curating and managing the authentic knowledge and thought artifacts developed *by students for students* is also reflective of transformational uses of technology. Obviously, this will look different for younger learners, who will need their teachers' help and support. What follows in Table 4.8 is a list of hosting sites that can be used to host your classroom's contributive website.

Blogs are wonderfully open-ended production and publication tools that allow anyone to produce and publish contributive knowledge products for an

TABLE 4.8 ■ **Technologies for Hosting and Curating Digital Contribution Products**

Task	Digital Tools	Cost
Students hosting and curating digital knowledge contribution products	Blogger.com	0
	edublogs.org	0
	Google Sites	0
	Kidblog.org	0
	Web.com	0
	Education.Weebly.com	0
	Wix.com	0
	WordPress.com	0
	SeeSaw.me	0
	Tumblr	0

authentic audience to view and use. Blogs are also well suited to multimedia content, enabling students to post text, images, videos, animations, and links to external sites of interest.

What's remarkable about these technologies is that students can create digital portfolio or process-folios that show the processes of progressions of knowledge representation over time. Students today can start to create knowledge portfolios as early as kindergarten and then use the same blog or wiki to capture their knowledge growth through the entirety of their public-school experiences. This is a powerful concept when one considers that today any student anywhere can create a sort of digital backpack of their knowledge gain using multimedia representations of their knowledge in a single, freely available cloud-based space. Never before have students had the ability to use such readily available process workspaces to capture and archive representative products of their thinking.

Because these blogs are cloud-based and stored in some external sites, students can use them to organize tutorials they create from their early primary-grade experiences all the way through high school, graduate school, and beyond. Never before in human history have learners been able to create and curate knowledge artifacts and the thinking journeys that underpin those artifacts for the purposes of the contribution of knowledge.

Unpacking the ways you think about and use digital tools to empower student contribution may once again prove helpful. Use the questions in Framing Tool T2.2 to help you think about how you use technology in your teaching, and be sure to notice the picture that emerges.

FRAMING TOOL T2.2
CONTRIBUTION

1. What are the digital tools that students use to contribute to the learning environment?

   _____

   _____

   _____

   _____

2. What are the tasks to which students apply those tools?

   _____

   _____

   _____

   _____

3. How does the use of those tools add value?

   _____

   _____

   _____

   _____

4. What other tasks do you think might be enhanced by digital contribution tools?

   _____

   _____

   _____

Available for download at **www.corwin.com/disruptiveclassroomtech**

Copyright © 2017 by Corwin. All rights reserved. Reprinted from *Disruptive Classroom Technologies: A Framework for Innovation in Education* by Sonny Magana. Thousand Oaks, CA: Corwin, www.corwin.com. Reproduction authorized only for the local school site or nonprofit organization that has purchased this book.

SUMMARY

The transformational uses of technology in education place students firmly at the center of classroom experiences. This shift is necessary to raise students' knowledge, consciousness, or mindsets to a new and superior state than that which existed prior to the learning experience. This is the essence of transformational learning experiences: we are no longer the same individuals at the completion of learning that is transformational. It is important, within the context of educational technology integration, to distinguish transformational from translational uses of technology in terms of the impact of each type of technology use on student learning. The difference is as striking as playing the same old songs around a campfire compared with rocking out like Chuck Berry.

The two stages of the T3 Framework discussed in this chapter—T2.1: Production and T2.2: Contribution—represent transformational uses of educational technology. The strategies offered in these two stages are illustrative of using technology in such a way that both the tasks and the students engaged in those tasks will become substantively changed by the use of digital tools. When implemented with reasonable fidelity, these strategies will measurably and reliably improve the quality and quantity of learning feedback. Improving the precision and timeliness of feedback makes this powerful process more actionable to students and serves to both inform and increase student learning performance and productivity (Hattie, 2009, 2012; Haystead & Magana, 2013; Haystead & Marzano, 2009a, 2010; Magana, 2016; Magana & Marzano, 2014, 2015).

> This is the essence of transformational learning experiences: we are no longer the same individuals at the completion of learning that is transformational.

Unleashing students' limitless learning potential ranks chief among all the noble, notable goals of education. Using educational technology with this intention in mind is a function of providing students with the experiences and resources that empower lifelong learning capacity by (1) producing mastery goals and engaging in ongoing growth and development toward mastery; (2) continuously monitoring and visualizing their progress toward mastery; (3) producing myriad ways of representing what they know, what they are able to do, and how they think about their knowledge and their thinking; and (4) applying their learning in a manner that is contributive and positively impacts the micro and macro community of learners.

Reframing the transformational uses of technology is a necessary second step toward realizing the much higher value added by the use of technology in the service of contributive teaching and learning. In the next chapter we will explore what may possibly yield the highest value added, through the final stage of the T3 Framework: transcendent uses of educational technology.

5 | T3: TRANSCENDENT TECHNOLOGY USE

T3: Transcendent

T2: Transformational

T3.1: Inquiry Design

T3.2: Social
Entrepreneurship

T1: Translational

T2.1: Production

T2.2: Contribution

T1.1: Automation

T1.2: Consumption

There's not much known about what's left to be discovered.

—Professor John Delaney

TRANSCENDENT TECHNOLOGY USE DEFINED

The origin of the word *transcend* can be found in the Latin word *transcendere*: to climb or to surmount. Experiences that are transcendent go well above and beyond the normal range of human outcomes and expectations. When one thinks of transcendent experiences, one imagines scaling unclimbed peaks, diving to uncharted depths, or accomplishing something else that has never been done. Transcendent experiences occur when we push hard against the edges of what is currently known, or possible, until we surmount those temporal limits and realize some new and superior level of performance. Humans have a long history of transcendent uses of technologies that not only disrupted previous ways of doing things but also enabled entirely new experiences and discoveries that far exceeded the prior known range of human expectations and limitations.

Eddie Van Halen's virtuosity represents the transcendent use of a modern technology, the electric guitar. Eddie was never satisfied with the status quo. He was always pushing the boundaries of what he knew by speculating on possible realities and then testing the outcomes and impact of his speculative thoughts. He not only surmounted the prior known limits of guitar playing, but he created an entirely original form of the music we know as rock and roll.

Eddie was a tinkerer. At a young age Eddie constantly asked the question most tinkerers ask: "What if?" For example, he was dissatisfied with the standard pickups in the Fender Stratocaster guitar, arguably one of the greatest musical instruments ever created. Eddie wondered what would happen if he took the humbucker pickup from a Gibson guitar and put it into a Stratocaster body. He was following an original line of inquiry, generating and testing resolutions to the problem as he went along, emboldened by the passion he had for making his guitar sound like none other. Over time and after multiple failures and iterations, Eddie created an entirely new instrument fueled by his own creativity, passion, and desire to tinker.

This proclivity continued throughout his life, and he developed his guitar artistry. During one fateful concert, Eddie was watching Led Zeppelin at the Los Angeles Forum. Legendary Led Zeppelin guitarist Jimmy Page used a finger-hammer technique, with his left hand on the guitar's neck and his right hand held in the air in exultation. This prompted Eddie to ask the question, "What if I use a finger hammer technique with not just one hand, but with both hands?" (Rothbard, 2015).

The rest is rock-and-roll history. Eddie's pioneering use of a double-handed finger hammer-on and pull-off technique on his newly created instrument yielded transcendent sounds. Not only were the task and the actor substantively changed, but Eddie also went far above the normal range of expectations and experience of the sounds that could be produced by an electric guitar. Aided of course by his virtuoso musicality, Eddie Van Halen surmounted what was previously known about playing rock-and-roll guitar, creating a new form of this iconic American music that was head and shoulders above anything music aficionados had ever heard.

In the context of teaching and learning, transcendent experiences are those experiences in which students, like Eddie Van Halen, achieve something well above and beyond the normal range of expectations, outcomes, and experiences in traditional classrooms. In addition to using technologies to automate tasks, consume information, produce knowledge artifacts, and contribute to the knowledge of others, transcendent technology use results in authentically original and unprecedented growth in knowledge, contribution, and value-generating performance.

A key driver of transcendent technology use is student passion. Students care very deeply about issues, situations, or problems that matter to them. This is particularly true in regard to social justice issues in which students desire to enact meaningful, ethical change or create something of value or benefit to the planet and its people. It can be argued that the things that matter to students matter the most in terms of engaging students in constructing and applying new knowledge and skills in ways that transcend common curriculum standards.

> Transcendent technology use results in authentically original and unprecedented growth in knowledge, contribution, and value-generating performance.

Students can begin this process by designing original lines of inquiry and software platforms to capture and share their learning journeys and accomplishments over time. Students generally only follow the learning maps generated by others. This can lead to a form of dependence; on the other hand, giving students the opportunity to forge new lines of inquiry and produce solutions in areas that matter to them allows students to transcend this dependence and acquire the tools, skills, and mindsets of independent and interdependent learning.

When students use technology in transcendent ways, they become their own curriculum mapmakers: cartographers of untrammeled knowledge landscapes, leaving a unique imprint for the benefit of posterity. Not only is this highly motivating and engaging, but it is reflective of how humans learn best: building on prior knowledge to make new connections between seemingly disparate phenomena to contextually and collectively generate understanding and meaning about ourselves and the interdependent, highly globalized world in which we live.

In the context of my teaching career, I have been fortunate to have many experiences in which students used technology in transcendent ways. One of the earliest occurred in 1993 as my science students at ACES Alternative High School were studying the phenomenon of global warming. I had a chance meeting with two local explorers, Helen and Bill Thayer, who spoke to our school community about their upcoming attempt to become the most senior couple to travel, alone and unaided, to the magnetic North Pole in March of 1994. At the time, Helen was 56 and her husband, Bill, was 67. Six years earlier, Helen Thayer had become the first woman to walk solo to the magnetic North Pole, pulling all her food and supplies in a tiny sled (Thayer, 1993).

I reasoned that creating a virtual adventure to the extremes of our planet would help contextualize the students' conceptual understanding of seasonal and systemic climate disruptions. I shared this seed of an idea with my students and they overwhelmingly agreed. They decided that they would use their newly acquired technology skills to share with an authentic global audience on the International Education and Resource Network (iEARN) the Thayers' inspirational messages, progress on their journey, and weather data, along with the results of their investigations on Arctic climate, animal life, and key elements of the trek. In essence, my students and I created the world's first global virtual field trip using new and emerging technology (Magana, 1994). Thousands of teachers and students in more than 20 countries took part in our virtual field trip to the magnetic North Pole!

My students named this venture the Polar Project and set about identifying and solving a raft of ill-structured problems that had never before been addressed—starting with the problem of how to bridge communication between our global partners on iEARN and the Thayers while the couple was alone on the Arctic ice. They came up with an elegant solution: As the Thayers would be using a high-frequency radio to make daily contact with their base camp in remote Resolute Bay in the Yukon Territory, my students resolved to figure out a way to get a dial-up Internet connection to the Thayers' base camp (this was in 1993 in the days before dial-up connections were commonplace). With my guidance, they went on an international quest of researching, e-mailing, and letter writing, resulting in donated access to the recently formed Canadian Pegasus Network. The sole request from network administrators was that we include Canadian schools in our e-mail dispatches from the Thayers during their trek—a request that my students gladly fulfilled.

My students exchanged daily e-mails with the base camp manager at Resolute Bay, who was in regular radio contact with the Thayers out on the frozen Arctic Ocean. We received updates on polar ice conditions, temperature, wind speed and direction, visibility, and animal sightings. Polar bears were a constant worry. We also tracked the Thayers' progress by charting their latitude and longitude coordinates on a map of the Arctic that hung in the front of my classroom. Every day my students would broadcast information about the Polar Project and their investigations on Arctic life through e-mail messages sent to a rapt global audience. They also created and published a daily newsletter, "The Arctic-le," to share their investigations with our local community.

Then, without warning, during the fourth week of their journey in late March of 1994, the Arctic Ice began to break apart nearly a month earlier than it had in recently recorded history, providing chilling evidence of global climate disruption. The resulting leads of frigid water became far too dangerous and prevented the Thayers from reaching their goal. Undaunted, the Thayers returned in late spring to a hero's welcome at ACES and immediately invited my students to serve as the global hub of their next adventure: a solo, unaided journey up the Amazon River into the heart of the Amazonian rain forest. My students and I began developing another virtual field trip dubbed the

Arctic to Amazon Project. By now my students and I were learning hypertext markup language (HTML), and we began publishing the Thayers' virtual field trip updates, their photographs, and their investigations on the flora and fauna of the Arctic and Amazon on the project website, which was hosted on the bourgeoning World Wide Web.

My classroom operated less like a traditional hierarchical learning environment and more like a small start-up company. I served as the learning manager while my students worked in small task-focused groups, contributing to the whole of the project by identifying outcomes, establishing workflows, delegating duties, and brainstorming ways to solve a raft of technical, communications, and outreach problems. They were generating and testing hypotheses on the fly and gaining real-time feedback to inform the quality of their decisions. They also created a brand-new platform, the virtual field trip, which won a Top 5% of the Web award in 1995 (Magana, 1994). Wielding new and emerging technologies to design this new platform, my students were able to engage in and apply the basic elements of entrepreneurial thinking: identifying a critical problem and generating multiple iterations of resolutions until they achieved their desired outcome. The value they generated by virtually exploring the world was inestimable, but we knew we were doing something no one had previously done. They were pioneers, knowledge cartographers constructing learning pathways on the "information superhighway" where none had previously existed.

These projects are illustrative of transcendent technology use. My students weren't just highly engaged—they were directing their own learning. Their use of e-mail, HTML, and the World Wide Web to engage a global audience in their investigations was not only transformational, but it went far above the normal range of prior experiences and expectations with classroom technologies. We disrupted the status quo by having students wrestle with ill-structured and ill-designed problems for which there were no existing solutions.

My students also used technology tools with heightened intentionality. They designed their own areas of inquiry focused on resolving a wicked problem they cared about deeply—global climate change. Through the Polar Project experiences, they learned that global climate disruption was an existential threat to the health and welfare of the planet a quarter of a century before it became popular tabloid and political fodder. They used new and emerging technologies to generate a global platform through which they were able to build a global community and contribute their knowledge about the fragility of our biosphere and the importance of greenhouse gas reduction. My students built one of the first websites dedicated to raising awareness of global climate change, habitat destruction, and the irreversible impact of biodiversity loss. These experiences clearly went above and beyond the normal range of classroom expectations and experiences and represent the transcendent stage of technology use in education.

This experience forever changed me as a teacher and as an educational technologist, because of our transcendent use of a new technology. This transcendent experience, and many others like it over the course of the past 24 years, started out with the question, "What if?" The transcendent potential of asking "What if?" cannot be overstated.

Thus, the two steps in the transcendent stage of educational technology use are T3.1: Inquiry Design and T3.2: Social Entrepreneurship. These two levels reflect ways students can leverage readily available technologies not only to become their own knowledge cartographers but to contribute something of value for the benefit of the planet and its people. This is the highest form of value added by educational technologies. The two steps of transcendent technology use, inquiry design and social entrepreneurship, will be discussed in the next sections.

T3.1: INQUIRY DESIGN

Students can begin engaging in transcendent uses of technology by designing learning journeys guided by their original lines of inquiry. It's important that for a period of time students follow maps and learning journeys that have sequential progressions of knowledge, but this process can and should be a scaffold toward independence and interdependence, not dependence. Knowledge that is built on previous knowledge is both a process of scaffolding—progressive reduction of instruction and guidance—and accretion—adding subsequent layers of knowing and meaning to one's foundational knowledge base.

It is of critical importance that students are given the opportunity to investigate problems that matter to them, design questions that address those problems, and then use the tools of research and inquiry to generate solutions to those problems. This is reflective of how research is conducted in the real world—specifically when investigators use a systematic approach to explore a particular problem that needs a solution (Gray, 2014). This process can be conducted, with proper guidance and support, at all grade levels in our school system. In the ensuing activities focused on struggling with ill-structured and unresolved problems that matter to them, students will learn a host of disciplines that will serve them, not only for the duration of the project but for a lifetime. This puts the learner squarely in the center of the learning experience. It is also illustrative of shifting students' roles from passive followers of curricula to active designers of personal mastery goals, cartographers of their own learning maps, and makers of the platforms and tools they need to navigate these new learning landscapes.

Once again, it might be helpful to consider the extent to which students' technology use represents the inquiry design stage by posing some guiding questions to help you think about and evaluate how you currently implement this stage of technology use. The guiding questions are listed in Table 5.1. These strategies are discussed in more detail in the following sections.

TABLE 5.1 ■ T3.1: Inquiry Design—Guiding Questions for Transcendent Technology Use

Guiding Question	Response		Value Indicator
1. Do students use technology to investigate a wicked real-life problem that matters to them?	Yes	No	Identifying relevant problems that ignite students' curiosity and passion
2. Do students use technology to design an original line of inquiry focused on generating a robust solution to the problem?	Yes	No	Creative ideation and investigation by posing the question "What if?"
3. Do students use technology to communicate, defend, and iterate their unique knowledge contribution to solve the problem?	Yes	No	Contributive iteration toward a more robust solution

T3.1-1: Students Use Technology to Investigate a Wicked Real-Life Problem That Matters to Them

Transcendent technology use begins with a wicked problem that matters to students. Unfortunately, there is no shortage of wicked problems that befall humanity on a daily basis. Fortunately, there are also no known limits to student creativity and imagination. Today's students are far more connected than any previous generation of learners, thanks in no small part to social media. There is a far greater likelihood now that many of these wicked problems will be well-known to students. Students actually care very deeply about the problems and injustices they see in the world around them and, unlike previous generations, may be in a greater position, in terms of their global and technological connectivity, to actually make the meaningful changes they wish to see in their world. That is why it is so important that students wrestle with ill-structured problems of their choosing rather than problems that are predetermined by their textbook or their teachers (Magana, Henly, Murphy, Rayl, & Travis, 1996).

A problem can be considered ill structured when it includes any of the following:

- A decision to be made
- A dilemma to be resolved
- A controversy to be resolved
- A process to be understood
- A mystery to be explained
- A choice to be made
- A product to be invented or created

Humans are naturally inquisitive problem solvers. However, it may be helpful to frame the process of inquiry design in a modern context. A reference to improving circumstances through creative problem solving can be found in the contemporary use of the term *hacking*. Hacking is, at its core, problem solving. But the modern use of the term has morphed from its earlier connotation, in which computer programmers breached security systems to gain access to unauthorized data, into a far more positive and creative application. Hacking is now more suggestive of a systemic and iterative approach to reviewing and reworking solutions to problems until robust, desirable outcomes are achieved (Barnes & Gonzales, 2015). Hackers are social engineers. They are tinkerers and makers who want to build a better world. Hackers are not as likely to passively accept the world as it is; rather, they actively seek to take apart and rebuild what they don't like about the world (Lacy, 2012).

High-tech companies routinely bring together programmers and engineers from disparate departments and work groups to engage in collaborative, open-ended hackathons. A hackathon is a robust, highly generative brainstorming session in which the collective power of the group is brought to bear on a worthy, ill-structured problem. Consider having students begin investigating a real-life problem by framing the work as a weekly hackathon in which student groups brainstorm and investigate a worthy, ill-structured wicked problem that matters to them.

The first elements of engaging in a hackathon focus on identifying an ill-structured problem that matters to students. This is an energizing, highly creative, although sometimes messy process, but one in which students' passion for solving a wicked problem is the key driver (Magana et al., 1996). These steps are shown in Table 5.2.

TABLE 5.2 ■ Steps for Problem Selection

Initial Inquiry Design Steps	Technology Tools
1. Brainstorm potential ill-structured, wicked real-life problems of concern to you, your school, or your community.	Google Class Microsoft Office 365 Microsoft OneNote MindJet Lucidchart
2. Build group consensus and select a problem that your group considers the highest priority.	Google Forms PollEverywhere Socrative
3. Define the dimensions of the problem by crafting a group problem statement.	Google Class Microsoft Office 365 Microsoft OneNote

Once students have generated consensus and selected a problem that needs a solution, it's important that they craft a problem statement. The problem statement should be written in such a way as to both clarify the problem *and* define the attributes of the desired outcomes or resolutions. The following sentence stem illustrates an incomplete problem statement:

How can we _____

(Describe the basic problem task[s] to be resolved)

in such a way that _____?

(List the attributes or conditions that must be considered)

The following are actual student-generated problem statements that were developed as part of the Illinois Student Project Information Network initiative (Magana et al., 1996):

From Prophetstown Elementary School:

"How can we <u>reduce, reuse, and recycle waste materials generated by the school</u>

(Describe the basic problem task[s] to be resolved)

in such a way that <u>is financially feasible and manageable within our time constraints?</u>"

(List the attributes or conditions that must be considered)

From Dheli Elementary School:

"How can we <u>develop community awareness of the problem contaminated lake water has upon our local groundwater supply</u>

(Describe the basic problem task[s] to be resolved)

in such a way that <u>(1) fosters community caring and involvement, (2) develops understanding of the importance of keeping groundwater as clean as possible, and (3) are within the budget set by the building principal?</u>"

(List the attributes or conditions that must be considered)

Crafting and communicating a clear problem statement that addresses the attributes of the desired resolutions will take some time, but it is a critical first step in the inquiry design process. The next step focuses on developing a methodology for investigating what is currently known about the problem and generating possible resolutions to the problem.

T3.1-2: Students Use Technology to Design
Original Inquiry and Generate Resolutions

It's important to honor prior knowledge and recognize those whose contributions enable our current areas of inquiry. The next step in the inquiry design/hackathon process is to have students use digital resources to research what is currently known about the problem. This involves investing, qualifying, and citing their sources of information and then synthesizing this knowledge into actionable solutions that address the problem. While graduate students are familiar with this process of reviewing the existing research literature, it's entirely possible to have student groups of all ages craft existing knowledge reviews using web search engines and online resources to gather information that reflects current knowledge regarding the problems.

Consider that the sum total of human knowledge is doubling about every year and that this rate will likely continue to increase until the total of human knowledge doubles in less than a day (Schilling, 2013). Now consider that much of that knowledge is made readily available in some digital format; so it's important to give students the opportunity to investigate a wide variety of digitized archival evidence to inform their knowledge reviews, including published research, graphic representations, video archives, expert testimonials, blogs, wikis, and podcasts. However, alongside authentic, verified digital knowledge and information, student research teams will also encounter reams of misinformation and willful obfuscation. It's important that students learn to triangulate information by gathering evidence from at least three different online sources, and then test the validity of their sources by examining them for bias and errors of reasoning (Magana & Marzano, 2014).

Use the scaffolds in Table 5.3 and Table 5.4 to help guide students' exploration of digital knowledge and determine the validity of their sources.

TABLE 5.3 ■ Common Reasoning Errors

Reasoning Error	Description
1. Faulty logic	Source presents conflicting or contradictory information, oversimplifies facts, argues for a claim by simply repeating the claim, or asserts something as wholly true that is only partly true.
2. Attack	Source rejects a claim by attacking the person or persons making the claim, or appeals to force.
3. Weak reference	Source reflects biases, presents little or no credible evidence, or makes appeals to authority, emotion, or popularity.
4. Misinformation	Source presents distorted or incorrect information, or incorrectly applies a broad generalization to support a claim.

Source: Adapted from Magana and Marzano (2014).

TABLE 5.4 ■ Knowledge Review Guide

1. What is the problem?		

2. What is the problem statement?		

3. What is known about the problem?	**Knowledge Source**	**Reasoning Errors** (3 = High, 2 = Medium, 1 = Low)
	1.	1. Faulty logic: 2. Weak reference: 3. Attack: 4. Misinformation:
	2.	1. Faulty logic: 2. Weak reference: 3. Attack: 4. Misinformation:
	3.	1. Faulty logic: 2. Weak reference: 3. Attack: 4. Misinformation:
4. What do we still need to know about the problem?	**Potential Knowledge Source**	**Reasoning Errors** (3 = High, 2 = Medium, 1 = Low)
	1.	1. Faulty logic: 2. Weak reference: 3. Attack: 4. Misinformation:
	2.	1. Faulty logic: 2. Weak reference: 3. Attack: 4. Misinformation:
	3.	1. Faulty logic: 2. Weak reference: 3. Attack: 4. Misinformation:

Available for download at **www.corwin.com/disruptiveclassroomtech**

Copyright © 2017 by Corwin. All rights reserved. Reprinted from *Disruptive Classroom Technologies: A Framework for Innovation in Education* by Sonny Magana. Thousand Oaks, CA: Corwin, www.corwin.com. Reproduction authorized only for the local school site or nonprofit organization that has purchased this book.

Table 5.3 presents an overview of common errors of reasoning that students can use as a lens to frame how they validate the sources of information. Use this guide to explicitly teach students what these common reasoning errors are, how they can identify examples of these errors in online sources, and how they might avoid them in their own reflection and analyses. Then have students use Table 5.4 to guide their knowledge review. When the students are investigating information sources that address the problem they are researching, have them use the lens of reasoning errors to code the level of errors they find in their information sources. Then, using this data, students can determine whether or not the information sources in question are reasonable, credible, and valid.

Once students have completed their knowledge reviews, they can begin to synthesize this knowledge into potential problem resolutions that meet the conditions of their problem statements. Have students use the technology tools in Table 5.4 to brainstorm and capture their thinking about potential resolutions to their problems. Then have students generate consensus to collectively determine which of those resolutions best fits the agreed-on conditions and constraints. These best-fitting resolutions will then become the students' tentative solutions to the problems that matter to them.

T3.1–3: Students Communicate, Defend, and Iterate Their Unique Knowledge Contribution

It's important that students present their findings to authentic problem stakeholders. These stakeholders can include but are not limited to their teachers and classmates, the larger school community, the broader community, and the global community of individuals or groups who may be directly or indirectly impacted by the problem and the resolutions students generate. Have students use the technology tools in Table 4.5 on page 51 to organize, digitize, and present their findings to their stakeholders, and then capture their presentations both for their own further review and to extend the robustness of their solutions through multiple iterations.

It's important that students actively reflect on their investigative experiences and deeply consider the new knowledge they have gained and contributed. When the students are communicating their solutions to stakeholders, have them respond to questions about their investigations to defend the strengths and recognize the weaknesses of their unique knowledge contributions to solve the problem. Moreover, have students identify possible errors of their own reasoning as well as potential biases that occurred during their investigations. Use the seven guiding questions in Table 5.5 on page 76 to help students engage in active reflection and ongoing iterations of their solutions to create a more robust solution.

Again, it may be useful to unpack the ways your students use digital tools to engage in the process of designing original lines of inquiry. Answer the questions in Framing Tool T3.1 to help you think about how your students use technology in this transcendent way, and then reflect on the picture that emerges.

FRAMING TOOL T3.1
INQUIRY DESIGN

1. What are the digital tools that your students use for inquiry design?

   _____

   _____

   _____

   _____

2. What are the tasks to which students apply those tools?

   _____

   _____

   _____

   _____

3. How does the use of those tools add value?

   _____

   _____

   _____

   _____

4. What other inquiry design tasks do you think might be enhanced by digital-production tools?

   _____

   _____

   _____

   _____

Available for download at **www.corwin.com/disruptiveclassroomtech**

Copyright © 2017 by Corwin. All rights reserved. Reprinted from *Disruptive Classroom Technologies: A Framework for Innovation in Education* by Sonny Magana. Thousand Oaks, CA: Corwin, www.corwin.com. Reproduction authorized only for the local school site or nonprofit organization that has purchased this book.

TABLE 5.5 ■ Guiding Reflection Questions

Guiding Questions

1. What is the problem and why is it important?

2. What did we hope would happen?

3. What did happen?

4. What were the strengths of our investigation? (Avoidance of reasoning errors and biases)

5. What were the weaknesses of our investigation? (Possible reasoning errors and biases)

6. What would we do differently?

7. What did we learn?

T3.2: SOCIAL ENTREPRENEURSHIP

This brings us to the final stage of transcendent technology use: social entrepreneurship. Social entrepreneurship combines generating social good and generating value (Shapiro, 2013). Engaging students in social entrepreneurship tasks builds on the inquiry design phase by contextualizing students' uses of technology tools into experiences that are driven by authentic passion and need. Social entrepreneurship activities may serve to unleash learners' latent leadership potential by framing the generation of value within the context of solving wicked problems that matter. Social entrepreneurs are currently hard at work pushing the edges of what is known by endeavoring to solve the numerous existential problems facing humans and the planet on which we live. They immerse themselves in the most intractable problem spaces to find robust solutions that improve the lives of others. It is this stage of technology use that potentially brings the highest degree of value—both to the learner and to the common good.

> Social entrepreneurship activities may serve to unleash learners' latent leadership potential by framing the generation of value within the context of solving wicked problems that matter.

Engaging in social entrepreneurship activities necessitates shifting students' role to that of autonomous creative thinkers who engage in solution ideation while wrestling with new, ill-structured problems for which there are not extant solutions—but for which there will need to be. This engenders more than students' owning their learning; they also become more deeply reflective, highly ethical agents of change for a better world. That's the highest value added by technology. The irony is that this is fundamentally a *human* rather than a technological value.

It is now possible in this third millennium to have students wield open-ended technology tools that go well above and beyond the prior range of expectations and experiences in schools. Students today can design new learning platforms and new tools within those learning environments, applying their newly designed tool sets and learning schema in an entrepreneurial fashion to either generate value or make a significant contribution to the health and welfare of the planet and its people. This makes for learning experiences that are powerful and meaningful.

Equipped with an understanding of modern software coding tools, students can readily explore uncharted knowledge frontiers while generating and testing hypotheses about new problem spaces in new ways (Magana & Marzano, 2014). However, it's important to consider that the development of modern coding environments, while already far more sophisticated than ever before, will continue to bring greater access and usability to these powerful design tools. A reasonable prediction can be made that in a short period of time, coding environments will become far easier to use. Much as the development of graphical user interfaces enabled enhanced software usability for the masses in the 1990s, future software environments will incorporate the use of visual object-oriented programming "code blocks." In time, this development may accelerate the need for learners to understand how to use coding tools for application, design, and self-expression, more than knowledge of coding language skills.

If this is even partially true, then a critical demand facing modern education will be the development of students' capacities for design, logic, and programmatic thinking. The set of essential and supplemental capacities for designing virtual environments with software is, and will continue to be, an engine of current and future economies in this third millennium. The current and emerging software-based economies are already generating enormous new value and potential to solve many of the greatest problems humans face today.

Once again, it might be helpful to consider the extent to which students' technology use represents the social entrepreneurship stage by posing some guiding questions that may help you think about and evaluate how you currently implement this stage of technology use. The guiding questions are listed in Table 5.6. These strategies are discussed in more detail in the following sections.

T3.2-1: Students Imagine, Design, and Create New Tools or Platforms to Solve Wicked Problems That Matter

It's important that students engage in the process of designing digital platforms and tools as a means to generate robust solutions to problems that matter. This will help ensure that a school's "Maker Space" does not become a "Faker Space," in which students make things without a meaningful purpose or merely follow tinkering recipes for making simple implements.

TABLE 5.6 ■ T3.2: Social Entrepreneurship—Guiding Questions for Transcendent Technology Use

Guiding Question	Response		Value Indicator
1. Do students imagine, design, and create new digital tools or platforms as solutions to wicked problems that matter?	Yes	No	Ideation of original solutions through rigorous struggle with wicked, ill-structured problems
2. Do students beta test, iterate, and generate robust versions of their digital solutions to wicked problems that matter?	Yes	No	Developing iterative resolutions aimed toward generating a more robust solution
3. Do students use digital tools to scale the implementation of their robust digital solutions to wicked problems that matter?	Yes	No	Implementing and scaling more robust solutions

Mitch Resnick, the director of the Media Lab at the Massachusetts Institute of Technology and the LEGO Papert Professor of Learning Research, developed a wonderfully generative and approachable problem-solving methodology: Lifelong Kindergarten. The four stages of this process are (1) imagine, (2) play, (3) share, and (4) reflect (Resnick, 2014). Mitch suggests that this is a process in which all humans naturally engage. He also suggests that, in the entirety of schooling, this four-step methodology is only regularly practiced in kindergarten. Unfortunately, once students graduate kindergarten, this natural process of learning is lost and they are tracked into curricula maps that are not of their own design. Once they are past kindergarten, there are very few opportunities for them to use their natural senses of wonder, imagination, and creativity through playing, sharing, and reflecting. In short, once students leave the kindergarten classroom, the opportunity to design new games, toys, or learning environments and experiences is unfortunately given very short shrift. It does not have to be this way.

Students need to imagine the solutions to a problem that matters to them, play with software tools to create these solutions, share their tools with collaborators, and then reflect on the merits and failings of their processes. Our ability to imagine, to dream up scenarios of applied digital ideas, is a uniquely human enterprise. We have to play with the ideas we design and share them with others to elicit understanding and collectively generate better solutions. Reflecting on our experiences in part and in totality provides critical feedback that drives the next iteration of a new imagination process.

This process of robust solution generation begins by firmly identifying the desired outcomes. This is best determined by compiling a list of leading indicators that reflect critical attributes of the desired outcomes. The more clearly they are communicated, the stronger the collective vision and commitment to achieve the vision. Have students work in groups to engage in an imagination brainstorm to dream up the desired outcome of their solution. Use the guiding questions in Table 5.7 to help them clearly develop how they see their new platform or tools resolving the wicked problem that matters to them.

> Our ability to imagine, to dream up scenarios of applied digital ideas, is a uniquely human enterprise.

Using freely available programming environments, students can begin to develop platforms, tools, and apps as solutions to wicked problems that matter. For example, students can use Scratch (www.scratch.mit.edu), the programming environment developed by Mitch Resnick and his team of educational epistemologists, to begin to design digital stories, games, or experiences that represent new ways to practice, deepen, apply, and speculate on new knowledge. Mitch and his colleagues perceive coding less as a list of technical skills and more as "a new type of literacy and personal expression, valuable for everyone, much like learning to write. We see coding as a new way for people to organize, express, and share their ideas" (Resnick & Siegel, 2015, para. 3).

Take for example the story of 11-year-old Mikaila Ulmer from Austin, Texas. The wicked problem that matters to Mikaila is the decimation of *Apis mellifera*—the honeybee. A condition known as colony collapse disorder has been annihilating the population of these apex pollinators across the planet, with potentially devastating effects on foods that require pollination; think about all the fruits, nuts, and vegetables that require bees to flourish (Morrison, 2013). Using social media and a variety of software tools, Mikaila applied her social entrepreneurship efforts by founding her own company, Me & the Bees

TABLE 5.7 ■ Guiding Questions for Solution Development

Guiding Questions
1. What is your problem statement?
2. What is the solution you are developing?
3. How will this solution add value?
4. What obstacles might impede your progress?
5. What are the indicators you will use to measure success?

Lemonade, featuring locally sourced honey. A portion of the profits from this successful venture is donated to philanthropic organizations dedicated to saving bees from extinction. Moreover, Mikaila continues to work toward the common good by building an app that will educate students around the world about the dangers facing honeybees and steps they can take to stop the bees' decline (Snapp, 2016).

Another moving example comes from Natalie Hampton, a 16-year-old from Sherman Oaks, California. The emotional and psychological damage caused by school bullying and isolation is the wicked social justice problem that matters to Natalie. After spending her entire seventh-grade year eating lunch alone in a cafeteria full of students, Natalie resolved to help other students avoid the pain of loneliness by creating Sit With Us, an app that helps shy students find a welcoming place to sit in their school cafeterias. Natalie is helping make the world a better place by using technology to transcend her own negative experiences while promoting a kinder and more inclusive school community (Wanshel, 2016).

Finally, one of my own students, Torrey Volk, exemplifies the ethos of social entrepreneurship. In 1996 I was honored to serve as Torrey's thesis chair as she was completing her master's in educational technology from City University in Seattle, Washington. A brilliant math teacher and coach, Torrey was determined to figure out how to leverage digital technologies to solve the wicked problem of helping *all* elementary school students master fundamental math skills. I was so moved by Torrey's dedication to the common good that we stayed in touch long after her successful thesis completion and defense. After years of pressing her original line of inquiry, and tinkering iteratively, Torrey launched MasterTrack, a cloud-based feedback system designed to help teachers and students set standards-based mastery learning goals and track students' growth and mastery in elementary math and English language arts. I am equally honored to serve as an advisor to Torrey's company, MasterTrack Solutions, as she is deeply committed to making the world a better place by improving the lives of elementary teachers and students.

These are but a few examples of what is possible by disrupting the current low-level use of educational technologies in our schools. There are no known limits to the potential that students, and teachers, have to make the world a better place. Striving to engage in transcendent technology use in our classrooms is clearly one way to realize this happy outcome. A good way to start is to consider how you and your students might use free open-ended developmental programming environments and app-building resources that will help students develop programmatic thinking, logic, and coding skills (see Table 5.8).

T3.2-2: Students Beta Test, Iterate, and Generate Robust Versions of Their Digital Solutions

Students will undoubtedly benefit from recognizing the importance of and tending to cycles of continuous growth and development. Rather than focusing

TABLE 5.8 ■ Educational Technologies for Learning Programming

Task	Digital Tools	Websites	Tool Category
Designing and creating new tools or platforms as solutions to wicked problems that matter	Adventure Game Studio	www.adventuregame studio.co.uk	Open-ended programming tools and environments
	Alice	www.alice.org	
	Code.org	www.code.org	
	CodeSpark	www.codespark.org	
	eToys	www.squeakland.org	
	KidsRuby	www.kidsruby.com	
	Love	www.love2d.org	
	NetLogo	ccl.northwestern.edu/netlogo	
	Processing	www.processing.org	
	Scratch	www.scratch.mit.edu	
	Scratch Junior	www.scratchjr.org	
Designing and creating new apps as solutions to wicked problems that matter	AppsBar	www.appsbar.com	Free app-building tools
	MIT AppInventor	www.appinventor.mit.edu	
	AppMakr4schools	www.appmakr4schools.com	
	Appypie	www.appypie.com	
	BuildFire	www.buildfire.com	

on building a one-time final version of their solutions, have students build a beta version of their solutions as a first iteration, test the impact by gathering feedback, and then use that feedback to inform the next iteration of their solutions. This is the tinkering stage of solution development, in which students continue to make changes to their solutions to improve functionality, usability, and accessibility. This process reflects the play phase of Lifelong Kindergarten (Resnick, 2014).

The phrase "Fail early and often" is a type of high-tech mantra heard in the hallways of start-up companies in Silicon Valley and beyond. What makes this thinking different is the prevailing perception of failure not as a disaster but as an opportunity for deeper reflective learning and iterative development. When it comes to digital solution development, failing often equals learning. The more failure students experience, the more opportunities they have for learning through debugging. When students begin building new platforms and tools as solutions to wicked problems that matter, consider guiding their perceptions so they begin to see failures in their digital solutions as opportunities for deeper learning and further development of more robust solutions.

> When it comes to digital solution development, failing often equals learning.

However, students should first identify the strengths of their solutions so they can begin with a foundation of positivity. Have students use the questions in Table 5.9 as a guide for the process of ongoing iterative reflection and development of their solutions to wicked problems that matter.

TABLE 5.9 ■ Guiding Questions for Iterative Reflection and Development

Guiding Questions

1. What outcome worked as well as or better than expected?
2. What outcome didn't work as well as expected?
3. What problems have you identified?
4. What are some possible resolutions to these problems?

T3.2-3: Students Scale the Implementation of Their Robust Digital Solutions

It's important that students share their solutions to wicked problems that matter with an authentic audience. This is the sharing stage of the Lifelong Kindergarten problem-solving methodology (Resnick, 2014). Students need to engage in the process of sharing their solutions and gathering feedback to inform their development and scale their solutions. Many of the coding and app-building tools listed in Table 5.8 support robust communities of practice. For example, students and teachers can also easily join the Scratch community of learners and share new ways to represent their Scratch solutions. Students from all over the world create Scratch experiences and are becoming designers of learning experiences that help them deepen their understanding of the content they are exploring, as well as their ability to design new software environments in which to make novel representations of their knowledge manifest.

The iEARN community is another wonderfully generative global community of learners who are committed to generating solutions to problems facing the planet and its people. While participation requires a nominal fee, the benefits students will gain from sharing and scaling student-generation solutions with the iEARN community are of exceedingly high value.

FRAMING TOOL T3.2
SOCIAL ENTREPRENEURSHIP

1. What are the digital tools that your students use for social entrepreneurship?

_____

_____

_____

_____

2. What are the tasks to which students apply those tools?

_____

_____

_____

_____

3. How does the use of those tools add value?

_____

_____

_____

_____

4. What other social entrepreneurship tasks do you think might be enhanced by digital tools?

_____

_____

_____

_____

Available for download at **www.corwin.com/disruptiveclassroomtech**

Copyright © 2017 by Corwin. All rights reserved. Reprinted from *Disruptive Classroom Technologies: A Framework for Innovation in Education* by Sonny Magana. Thousand Oaks, CA: Corwin, www.corwin.com. Reproduction authorized only for the local school site or nonprofit organization that has purchased this book.

It may also benefit students to solicit input on their digital solutions by harnessing the potential collective interest using social media tools. Consider having students develop a social presence by producing blogs, wikis, or podcasts to share their solutions with an authentic global audience. Have students harness the broadcasting potential of Twitter, Facebook, and other social media tools to share and scale their solutions while engaging in continuous cycles of implementation, reflection, and iteration.

Finally, consider having students explore additional resources for developing their social entrepreneurship skills. One helpful activity may be to have students connect with other social entrepreneurs. For example, have students explore Ashoka (www.ashoka.org), a global organization dedicated to identifying and promoting leading social entrepreneurs. With grant and mentorship opportunities available, Ashoka may help students unleash their potential to better investigate, understand, and solve wicked problems that matter to them.

Again, it may be useful to unpack the ways your students use digital tools to engage in the process of social entrepreneurship. Answer the questions in Framing Tool T3.2 on the previous page to help you think about how your students use technology in this transcendent way, and then reflect on the picture that emerges.

SUMMARY

Transcendent use of educational technology tools places wicked problems that matter to students at the center of the learning experience. Moreover, transcendent uses of educational technologies go above and beyond the current range of experiences and expectations within classroom learning environments. While these types of learning experiences with technology are well within the reach of teachers and students, they are generally seen as exceptional. However, that exceptionality rests in the manner in which individuals wield those technologies; more specifically, the potential for transcendent application of educational technologies is made manifest when students engage their innate capacity to imagine, play, share, and reflect (Resnick, 2014). One of the most important ways humans have been able to speculate and transcend experience is by continuously posing the exceedingly powerful open-ended question, "What if?"

The two stages of the T3 Framework discussed in this chapter—T3.1: Inquiry Design and T3.2: Social Entrepreneurship—represent transcendent uses of educational technology. The strategies offered in these two stages are illustrative of using technology in such a way that not only are the tasks and the students engaged in those tasks substantively changed by the use of digital tools, but the experiences gained go far above and beyond known ranges of experience and expectations. This level of technology use is predicated on students serving as the main drivers of both their learning and their capacities as digital toolmakers. The first step is to give students the opportunity to express their caring about a condition they wish to change, a wicked problem they want to solve, or a social justice issue that needs to be addressed and corrected.

As so little is known about what's left to be discovered (Delaney, 2015), there are no known limits regarding what students will discover when solving problems about which they are passionate. Limitless learning potential is a preexisting condition for all humans. Humans have evolved to our present state because of our evolutionary disposition to generate, apply, and communicate new knowledge. This process, though, is not without hardship. It engenders struggle, failure, more failure, and learning from that failure.

The new generation of ideation will take the form of digital tinkerers in the third millennium. As educators, it is our moral, ethical, and professional responsibility to provide these students with equitable opportunities to learn how to become inquirers and problem solvers—cartographers of new knowledge landscapes equipped with the skills and resources they need to become their own learning toolmakers. The time to start is now.

Putting the T3 Framework to Use

6 APPLYING THE T3 FRAMEWORK

So this is my aim for watercooler conversations: improve
the ability to identify and understand errors of judgment and
choice, in others and eventually in ourselves, by providing
a richer and more precise language to discuss them.

—Daniel Kahneman

As you think about how you are currently using the elements in the T3 Framework in your instructional practices, ask yourself if you are engaged in translational technology use, transformational technology use, or transcendent technology use. Perhaps you are squarely within the realm of one stage or are between stages. The point is that the stage in which you are currently operating matters less than demonstrated progress and growth. Just like Eddie Van Halen told me over the radio so many years ago, you may be perfectly happy playing the same songs around the campfire, but if you want to get better, you have to realize that you are at a certain stage and that pathways exist for you to experience other stages of proficiency. What matters more is that you know where you are in the T3 Framework and that you invest effort to move to a new, higher level, whatever that new level may be.

USING THE T3 FRAMEWORK FOR SELF-ASSESSMENT, GOAL SETTING, AND CONTINUOUS PERSONAL GROWTH

To engage in the process of becoming a deeply reflective, modern practitioner, teachers should set professional growth goals for each year of their teaching careers (Marzano, 2012). This will help ensure that teachers engage in ongoing cycles of continuous growth and mastery in their classroom practices. The purpose of this chapter is to provide teachers and their evaluating administrators with guidance as to how to collaboratively self-assess, plan, and evaluate the implementation of the three stages of the T3 Framework—T1: Translational Technology Use, T2: Transformational Technology Use, and T3: Transcendent Technology Use.

It would be helpful for teachers to use a proficiency scale to reflect on their current levels of technology use. Using a nominal scale can also support teachers in setting goals and, more important, monitoring and tracking their progress toward those goals with greater precision. Such proficiency scales are associated with clear, unambiguous feedback and large growth gains (Fuchs & Fuchs, 1986; Hattie, 2009; Magana & Marzano, 2014; Marzano, 2007).

To be even more specific, there are two categories of reflection: reflection-on-action and reflection-in-action. Reflection-on-action occurs at the completion of some task or performance, while reflection-in-action is conducted during the performance of a task (Schön, 1983). While both are important, it is the latter, reflection-in-action, that appears to have the greatest potential for generating improvements in instructional practice through the development of improvisational skills and discernment "in the moment" (Kahneman, 2011). Highly skilled educators reach that level because they develop capacities to mindfully tend to both their practices and the impact of their instructional decisions on their students' academic and social well-being in the moment.

An important first step in this process is to engage in a self-audit to frame the "here and now" of their practices and then establish meaningful yearly growth goals. What will help teachers engage in reflective self-audits is a proficiency scale to aid in their determination of their levels of competence. To be highly usable and actionable, such a scale should be clear, precise, and contain only three points of competence. Humans are able to agilely gauge the qualities of phenomena we experience using a simple qualitative coding protocol, such as (1) low, (2) medium, and (3) high (Gray, 2014). Adding additional stages runs the risk of rendering the scale less usable as a reflection-in-action tool. Thus, a proficiency scale with only three numerical increments may be more readily adaptable to guiding teachers' everyday classroom reflection-in-action.

The T3 Framework is designed to be both compact and actionable. Using a three-point proficiency scale seems a reasonable way to aid teachers as they engage in reflection-in-action during their instruction. This scale will also be helpful to support teachers and administrators as they jointly engage in reflection-on-action upon the completion of a lesson that was observed for evaluation purposes. A highly usable three-point teacher proficiency scale is shown in Table 6.1.

With these incremental stages clearly in mind, teachers can then engage in self-assessments on their capacities with each element in the T2: Transformational Technology Use and T3: Transcendent Technology Use phases. A reproducible guide for the task of teacher self-assessment is shown in Table 6.2. It should be noted that the critical stages of T2 and T3 have guiding elements, while the entry-level stage of T1 consists of questions to guide teachers' self-assessments of a wide variety of digital automation and consumption tools.

TABLE 6.1 ■ Three-Point Teacher Proficiency Scale

1. Beginning	2. Developing	3. Mastering
Not yet nearing agile, adaptive use of digital tools to enhance teaching and learning tasks that demonstrates little or no impact monitoring and critical errors or oversights	Nearing agile, adaptive use of digital tools to enhance teaching and learning tasks that demonstrates some impact monitoring and some critical errors or oversights	Agile, adaptive use of digital tools to enhance teaching and learning tasks that demonstrates impact mindfulness and is free from critical errors or oversights

TABLE 6.2 ■ Teacher Self-Assessment Guide for T3 Framework

T3 Level	Proficiency Scale		
	1. Beginning	**2. Developing**	**3. Mastering**
	Not yet nearing agile, adaptive use of digital tools to enhance teaching and learning tasks that demonstrates little or no impact monitoring and critical errors or oversights	Nearing agile, adaptive use of digital tools to enhance teaching and learning tasks that demonstrates some impact monitoring and some critical errors or oversights	Agile, adaptive use of digital tools to enhance teaching and learning tasks that demonstrates impact mindfulness and is free from critical errors or oversights

T1.1: Automation

What do I do, or have students do, to use digital tools to automate teaching and learning tasks to increase efficiency, productivity, and reduce errors?

Digital Tool	1. Beginning	2. Developing	3. Mastering
1.			
2.			
3.			

(Continued)

TABLE 6.2 ■ (Continued)

T1.2: Consumption

What do I do, or have students do, to use digital tools to consume instructional and learning information and media to increase access, efficiency, and productivity?

Digital Tool	1. Beginning	2. Developing	3. Mastering
1.			
2.			
3.			

T2.1: Production

What do I do, or have students do, to use digital tools to produce learning artifacts that show what students know, show what they are able to do, and make their thinking explicit?

	1. Beginning	2. Developing	3. Mastering
T2.1–1: Students use digital tools to produce, review, archive, and update personal mastery goals			
T2.1–2: Students use digital tools to continuously track and visualize their progress toward their mastery goals			
T2.1–3: Students use digital tools to produce, archive, and review authentic knowledge and thought artifacts			

T2.2: Contribution

What do I do, or have students do, to use digital tools to produce learning artifacts that are designed to contribute to the learning of others?

	1. Beginning	2. Developing	3. Mastering
T2.2–1: Students use digital tools to contribute to and track their observance of classroom promises and commitments			

T2.2–2: Students use digital tools to produce authentic tutorials designed to contribute to others' learning			
T2.2–3: Students use digital tools to curate their authentic learning tutorials			

T3.1: Inquiry Design

What do I do, or have students do, to use digital tools to press an original line of inquiry to resolve a wicked problem that matters to them?

	1. Beginning	2. Developing	3. Mastering
T3.1–1: Students use digital tools to investigate a wicked real-life problem that matters to them			
T3.1–2: Students use digital tools to design an original line of inquiry focused on generating a robust solution to a wicked problem that matters			
T3.1–3: Students use technology to communicate, defend, and iterate their unique knowledge contribution to solve the wicked problem			

T3.2: Social Entrepreneurship

What do I do, or have students do, to use digital tools to engage in the iterative process of creating a more robust solution to a wicked problem that matters to them?

	1. Beginning	2. Developing	3. Mastering
T3.2–1: Students imagine, design, and create new digital tools or platforms as solutions to wicked problems that matter			

(Continued)

TABLE 6.2 ■ (Continued)

	1. Beginning	2. Developing	3. Mastering
T3.2–2: Students beta test, iterate, and generate robust versions of their digital solutions to wicked problems that matter			
T3.2–3: Students use digital tools to scale the implementation of their robust digital solutions to wicked problems that matter			

Available for download at **www.corwin.com/disruptiveclassroomtech**

Copyright © 2017 by Corwin. All rights reserved. Reprinted from *Disruptive Classroom Technologies: A Framework for Innovation in Education* by Sonny Magana. Thousand Oaks, CA: Corwin, www.corwin.com. Reproduction authorized only for the local school site or nonprofit organization that has purchased this book.

The next step is for educators to establish and communicate precise goals for professional growth. I recommend that teachers do this in collaboration with their building principals, instructional leadership teams, or professional learning communities (PLCs) or instructional coaches. This will help everyone in a learning community develop, maintain, and enhance a common language of modern instruction with modern tools. To be of the greatest help, these goals should be (1) precise, (2) measurable, and (3) actionable. The process of professional goal setting can be done individually, with colleagues in PLCs (DuFour & Eaker, 1998) or with an evaluating administrator. Teachers can use the guiding prompts in Table 6.3 through Table 6.8 to support their development of precise, measurable, and actionable professional growth goals that are reflective of each stage in the T3 Framework. As there are multiple entry points—and many roads to Rome—anyone using the T3 Framework should begin by self-assessing his or her entry point and then making intentional steps for continuous growth and mastery.

Translational Technology Use

TABLE 6.3 ■ Professional Goal-Setting Guide for T1.1: Automation	
T1.1: Automation	**Prompt**
3. Mastering Agile, adaptive use of digital tools to enhance teaching and learning tasks that demonstrates impact mindfulness and is free from critical errors or oversights	I will demonstrate mastering my use of _____ _____ to automate the task of (Digital tool) _____ by _____. (Teaching or learning task) (Date)
2. Developing Nearing agile, adaptive use of digital tools to enhance teaching and learning tasks that demonstrates some impact monitoring and some errors or oversights	I will demonstrate developing my use of _____ _____ to automate the task of (Digital tool) _____ by _____. (Teaching or learning task) (Date)
1. Beginning Not yet nearing agile, adaptive use of digital tools to enhance teaching and learning tasks that demonstrates little or no impact monitoring and critical errors or oversights	I will demonstrate beginning my use of _____ _____ to automate the task of (Digital tool) _____ by _____. (Teaching or learning task) (Date)

Available for download at **www.corwin.com/disruptiveclassroomtech**

Copyright © 2017 by Corwin. All rights reserved. Reprinted from *Disruptive Classroom Technologies: A Framework for Innovation in Education* by Sonny Magana. Thousand Oaks, CA: Corwin, www.corwin.com. Reproduction authorized only for the local school site or nonprofit organization that has purchased this book.

TABLE 6.4 ■ Professional Goal-Setting Guide for T1.2: Consumption

T1.2: Consumption	Prompt

3. Mastering
 	
Agile, adaptive use of digital tools to enhance teaching and learning tasks that demonstrates impact mindfulness and is free from critical errors or oversights
	I will demonstrate mastering my use of _____
	
	_____ to consume digital
	        (Digital tool)
	media to benefit the task of _____
	
	_____ by _____.
	    (Teaching or learning task) (Date)

2. Developing
 	
Nearing agile, adaptive use of digital tools to enhance teaching and learning tasks that demonstrates some impact monitoring and some errors or oversights
	I will demonstrate developing my use of _____
	
	_____ to consume digital
	        (Digital tool)
	media to benefit the task of _____
	
	_____ by _____.
	    (Teaching or learning task) (Date)

1. Beginning
 	
Not yet nearing agile, adaptive use of digital tools to enhance teaching and learning tasks that demonstrates little or no impact monitoring and critical errors or oversights
	I will demonstrate beginning my use of _____
	
	_____ to consume digital
	        (Digital tool)
	media to benefit the task of _____
	
	_____ by _____.
	    (Teaching or learning task) (Date)

Available for download at **www.corwin.com/disruptiveclassroomtech**

Copyright © 2017 by Corwin. All rights reserved. Reprinted from *Disruptive Classroom Technologies: A Framework for Innovation in Education* by Sonny Magana. Thousand Oaks, CA: Corwin, www.corwin.com. Reproduction authorized only for the local school site or nonprofit organization that has purchased this book.

Transformational Technology Use

TABLE 6.5 ■ Professional Goal-Setting Guide for T2.1: Production	
T2.1: Production	**Prompt**
3. Mastering Agile, adaptive use of digital tools to enhance teaching and learning tasks that demonstrates impact mindfulness and is free from critical errors or oversights	I will demonstrate mastering my integration of _____ _____ to support students (Digital tool) engaging in the production task of _____ _____ (Insert student production task T2.1–1, T2.1–2, or T2.1–3) by _____. (Date)
2. Developing Nearing agile, adaptive use of digital tools to enhance teaching and learning tasks that demonstrates some impact monitoring and some errors or oversights	I will demonstrate developing my integration of _____ _____ to support students (Digital tool) engaging in the production task of _____ _____ (Insert student production task T2.1–1, T2.1–2, or T2.1–3) by _____. (Date)
1. Beginning Not yet nearing agile, adaptive use of digital tools to enhance teaching and learning tasks that demonstrates little or no impact monitoring and critical errors or oversights	I will demonstrate beginning my integration of _____ _____ to support students (Digital tool) engaging in the production task of _____ _____ (Insert student production task T2.1–1, T2.1–2, or T2.1–3) by _____. (Date)

Available for download at **www.corwin.com/disruptiveclassroomtech**

Copyright © 2017 by Corwin. All rights reserved. Reprinted from *Disruptive Classroom Technologies: A Framework for Innovation in Education* by Sonny Magana. Thousand Oaks, CA: Corwin, www.corwin.com. Reproduction authorized only for the local school site or nonprofit organization that has purchased this book.

TABLE 6.6 ■ Professional Goal-Setting Guide for T2.2: Contribution

T2.2: Contribution	Prompt
3. Mastering Agile, adaptive use of digital tools to enhance teaching and learning tasks that demonstrates impact mindfulness and is free from critical errors or oversights	I will demonstrate mastering my integration of _____ _____ to support students (Digital tool) engaging in the contribution task of _____ _____ (Insert student contribution task T2.2–1, T2.2–2, or T2.2–3) by _____. (Date)
2. Developing Nearing agile, adaptive use of digital tools to enhance teaching and learning tasks that demonstrates some impact monitoring and some errors or oversights	I will demonstrate developing my integration of _____ _____ to support students (Digital tool) engaging in the contribution task of _____ _____ (Insert student contribution task T2.2–1, T2.2–2, or T2.2–3) by _____. (Date)
1. Beginning Not yet nearing agile, adaptive use of digital tools to enhance teaching and learning tasks that demonstrates little or no impact monitoring and critical errors or oversights	I will demonstrate beginning my integration of _____ _____ to support students (Digital tool) engaging in the contribution task of _____ _____ (Insert student contribution task T2.2–1, T2.2–2, or T2.2–3) by _____. (Date)

Available for download at **www.corwin.com/disruptiveclassroomtech**

Copyright © 2017 by Corwin. All rights reserved. Reprinted from *Disruptive Classroom Technologies: A Framework for Innovation in Education* by Sonny Magana. Thousand Oaks, CA: Corwin, www.corwin.com. Reproduction authorized only for the local school site or nonprofit organization that has purchased this book.

Transcendent Technology Use

TABLE 6.7 ■ Professional Goal-Setting Guide for T3.1: Inquiry Design	
T3.1: Inquiry Design	**Prompt**
3. Mastering Agile, adaptive use of digital tools to enhance teaching and learning tasks that demonstrates impact mindfulness and is free from critical errors or oversights	I will demonstrate mastering my integration of _____ _____ to support students <div align=center>(Digital tool)</div>engaging in the inquiry design task of _____ _____ (Insert student inquiry design task T3.1–1, T3.1–2, or T3.1–3) by _____. <div align=center>(Date)</div>
2. Developing Nearing agile, adaptive use of digital tools to enhance teaching and learning tasks that demonstrates some impact monitoring and some errors or oversights	I will demonstrate developing my integration of _____ _____ to support students <div align=center>(Digital tool)</div>engaging in the inquiry design task of _____ _____ (Insert student inquiry design task T3.1–1, T3.1–2, or T3.1–3) by _____. <div align=center>(Date)</div>
1. Beginning Not yet nearing agile, adaptive use of digital tools to enhance teaching and learning tasks that demonstrates little or no impact monitoring and critical errors or oversights	I will demonstrate beginning my integration of _____ _____ to support students <div align=center>(Digital tool)</div>engaging in the inquiry design task of _____ _____ (Insert student inquiry design task T3.1–1, T3.1–2, or T3.1–3) by _____. <div align=center>(Date)</div>

Available for download at **www.corwin.com/disruptiveclassroomtech**

Copyright © 2017 by Corwin. All rights reserved. Reprinted from *Disruptive Classroom Technologies: A Framework for Innovation in Education* by Sonny Magana. Thousand Oaks, CA: Corwin, www.corwin.com. Reproduction authorized only for the local school site or nonprofit organization that has purchased this book.

TABLE 6.8 ■ Professional Goal-Setting Guide for T3.2: Social Entrepreneurship	

T3.2: Social Entrepreneurship	Prompt
3. Mastering Agile, adaptive use of digital tools to enhance teaching and learning tasks that demonstrates impact mindfulness and is free from critical errors or oversights	I will demonstrate mastering my integration of _____ _____ to support students (Digital tool) engaging in the social entrepreneurship task of _____ _____ (Insert social entrepreneurship task T3.2–1, T3.2–2, or T3.2–3) by _____. (Date)
2. Developing Nearing agile, adaptive use of digital tools to enhance teaching and learning tasks that demonstrates some impact monitoring and some errors or oversights	I will demonstrate developing my integration of _____ _____ to support students (Digital tool) engaging in the social entrepreneurship task of _____ _____ (Insert social entrepreneurship task T3.2–1, T3.2–2, or T3.2–3) by _____. (Date)
1. Beginning Not yet nearing agile, adaptive use of digital tools to enhance teaching and learning tasks that demonstrates little or no impact monitoring and critical errors or oversights	I will demonstrate beginning my integration of _____ _____ to support students (Digital tool) engaging in the social entrepreneurship task of _____ _____ (Insert social entrepreneurship task T3.2–1, T3.2–2, or T3.2–3) by _____. (Date)

Available for download at **www.corwin.com/disruptiveclassroomtech**

Copyright © 2017 by Corwin. All rights reserved. Reprinted from *Disruptive Classroom Technologies: A Framework for Innovation in Education* by Sonny Magana. Thousand Oaks, CA: Corwin, www.corwin.com. Reproduction authorized only for the local school site or nonprofit organization that has purchased this book.

USING THE T3 FRAMEWORK
FOR TEACHER EVALUATION

While it's important for teachers to set clear professional growth goals, it is equally important for teachers to reflect on, monitor, and evaluate their progress toward professional growth and mastery goals with an administrator through classroom observations. This is a process that can be enhanced by using precise guidelines and indicators for each stage of technology use in the T3 Framework. Evaluating administrators and teachers can use Table 6.9 through Table 6.14 to guide and support teachers through more precise, measurable, and actionable evaluation practices focused on the integration of digital tools to enhance teaching and learning.

Translational Technology Use

A guide for evaluating teachers' integration of digital tools for the translational technology use stage T1.1: Automation is shown in Table 6.9. Consider using this guide to support teachers as they increase their competence and proficiency in this stage of technology integration. Again, anyone using the T3 Framework should ideally first identify the stage that corresponds with his or her initial self-assessment and then take intentional steps to continuously grow from that point forward. Note the inclusion of indicators for both teacher and student use of digital tools to enhance automation tasks.

A guide for evaluating teachers' integration of digital tools for the translational technology use stage T1.2: Consumption is shown in Table 6.10. Consider using this guide to support teachers as they increase their competence and proficiency in this stage of technology integration. Again, please note the inclusion of indicators for both teacher and student use of digital tools to enhance consumption tasks.

Transformational Technology Use

A guide for evaluating teachers' integration of digital tools for the transformational technology use stage T2.1: Production is shown in Table 6.11. Consider using this guide to support teachers as they increase their competence and proficiency in this stage of technology integration. Note the inclusion of indicators for both teacher and student use of digital tools to enhance production tasks.

A guide for evaluating teachers' integration of digital tools for the transformational technology use stage T2.2: Contribution is shown in Table 6.12. Consider using this guide to support teachers as they increase their competence and proficiency in this stage of technology integration. Note the inclusion of indicators for both teacher and student use of digital tools to enhance contribution tasks.

TABLE 6.9 ■ T1.1: Automation—Teacher Observation Guide

T1.1: Automation

What do I do, or have students do, to automate teaching and learning tasks with digital tools to save time, increase efficiency, and reduce errors?

The teacher uses digital tools to save time and increase efficiency and accuracy of instructional or learning tasks.	**Notes**
Teacher Evidence	**Student Evidence**
☐ Teacher use of digital tools results in increased time savings during administrative or teaching tasks. ☐ Teacher use of digital tools results in increased efficiency when completing administrative or teaching tasks. ☐ Teacher use of digital tools results in increased accuracy of administrative or teaching tasks (error reduction).	☐ Student use of digital tools results in increased time savings during learning tasks. ☐ Student use of digital tools results in increased efficiency during learning tasks. ☐ Student use of digital tools results in increased accuracy during learning tasks (error reduction).

Proficiency Scale (Use evidence checkpoints to determine level of proficiency.)

1. Beginning	2. Developing	3. Mastering
Not yet nearing agile, adaptive use of digital tools to enhance teaching and learning tasks that demonstrates little or no impact monitoring and critical errors or oversights	Nearing agile, adaptive use of digital tools to enhance teaching and learning tasks that demonstrates some impact monitoring and some critical errors or oversights	Agile, adaptive use of digital tools to enhance teaching and learning tasks that demonstrates impact mindfulness and is free from critical errors or oversights

Available for download at **www.corwin.com/disruptiveclassroomtech**

Copyright © 2017 by Corwin. All rights reserved. Reprinted from *Disruptive Classroom Technologies: A Framework for Innovation in Education* by Sonny Magana. Thousand Oaks, CA: Corwin, www.corwin.com. Reproduction authorized only for the local school site or nonprofit organization that has purchased this book.

TABLE 6.10 ■ T1.2: Consumption—Teacher Observation Guide

T1.2: Consumption

What do I do, or have students do, to consume content-related knowledge and information with digital tools?

The teacher uses digital tools to increase access, save time, and increase consumption of content knowledge and information.	**Notes**
Teacher Evidence	**Student Evidence**
☐ Teacher use of digital tools results in increased access to content knowledge and information during administrative or teaching tasks. ☐ Teacher use of digital tools for consumption of content knowledge and information results in increased time savings during administrative or teaching tasks. ☐ Teacher use of digital tools results in increased consumption of content knowledge and information during administrative or teaching tasks.	☐ Student use of digital tools results in increased access to content knowledge and information during learning tasks. ☐ Student use of digital tools results in increased time savings while consuming content knowledge and information during learning tasks. ☐ Student use of digital tools results in increased consumption of content knowledge and information during learning tasks.

Proficiency Scale (Use evidence checkpoints to determine level of proficiency.)

1. Beginning	2. Developing	3. Mastering
Not yet nearing agile, adaptive use of digital tools to enhance teaching and learning tasks that demonstrates little or no impact monitoring and critical errors or oversights	Nearing agile, adaptive use of digital tools to enhance teaching and learning tasks that demonstrates some impact monitoring and some critical errors or oversights	Agile, adaptive use of digital tools to enhance teaching and learning tasks that demonstrates impact mindfulness and is free from critical errors or oversights

Available for download at **www.corwin.com/disruptiveclassroomtech**

Copyright © 2017 by Corwin. All rights reserved. Reprinted from *Disruptive Classroom Technologies: A Framework for Innovation in Education* by Sonny Magana. Thousand Oaks, CA: Corwin, www.corwin.com. Reproduction authorized only for the local school site or nonprofit organization that has purchased this book.

TABLE 6.11 ■ T2.1: Production—Teacher Observation Guide

T2.1: Production

What do I do to have students use digital tools for production during learning tasks?

The teacher facilitates students' use of digital tools to enhance production during learning tasks.	**Notes**
Teacher Evidence	**Student Evidence**
☐ Teacher facilitates students' use of digital tools to produce, review, archive, and update personal mastery goals.	☐ Students use digital tools to produce, review, archive, and update personal mastery goals.
☐ Teacher facilitates students' use of digital tools to continuously track and visualize their growth toward their mastery goals.	☐ Students use digital tools to continuously track and visualize their growth toward their mastery goals.
☐ Teacher facilitates students' use of digital tools to produce, archive, and review authentic knowledge artifacts that represent what students know and are able to do while making their thinking explicit.	☐ Students use digital tools to produce, archive, and review authentic knowledge artifacts that represent what they know and are able to do while making their thinking explicit.

Proficiency Scale (Use evidence checkpoints to determine level of proficiency.)

1. Beginning	2. Developing	3. Mastering
Not yet nearing agile, adaptive use of digital tools to enhance teaching and learning tasks that demonstrates little or no impact monitoring and critical errors or oversights	Nearing agile, adaptive use of digital tools to enhance teaching and learning tasks that demonstrates some impact monitoring and some critical errors or oversights	Agile, adaptive use of digital tools to enhance teaching and learning tasks that demonstrates impact mindfulness and is free from critical errors or oversights

Available for download at **www.corwin.com/disruptiveclassroomtech**

Copyright © 2017 by Corwin. All rights reserved. Reprinted from *Disruptive Classroom Technologies: A Framework for Innovation in Education* by Sonny Magana. Thousand Oaks, CA: Corwin, www.corwin.com. Reproduction authorized only for the local school site or nonprofit organization that has purchased this book.

TABLE 6.12 ■ T2.2: Contribution—Teacher Observation Guide

T2.2: Contribution

What do I do to have students use digital tools for contribution during learning tasks?

The teacher facilitates students' use of digital tools to enhance contribution during learning tasks.	**Notes**
Teacher Evidence	**Student Evidence**
☐ Teacher facilitates students' use of digital tools to contribute to and track their observance of classroom promises and commitments. ☐ Teacher facilitates students' use of digital tools to produce authentic tutorials designed to contribute to others' learning. ☐ Teacher facilitates students' use of digital tools to curate their authentic learning tutorials.	☐ Students use digital tools to contribute to and track their observance of classroom promises and commitments. ☐ Students use digital tools to produce authentic tutorials designed to contribute to others' learning. ☐ Students use digital tools to curate their authentic learning tutorials.

Proficiency Scale (Use evidence checkpoints to determine level of proficiency.)

1. Beginning	2. Developing	3. Mastering
Not yet nearing agile, adaptive use of digital tools to enhance teaching and learning tasks that demonstrates little or no impact monitoring and critical errors or oversights	Nearing agile, adaptive use of digital tools to enhance teaching and learning tasks that demonstrates some impact monitoring and some critical errors or oversights	Agile, adaptive use of digital tools to enhance teaching and learning tasks that demonstrates impact mindfulness and is free from critical errors or oversights

Available for download at **www.corwin.com/disruptiveclassroomtech**

Copyright © 2017 by Corwin. All rights reserved. Reprinted from *Disruptive Classroom Technologies: A Framework for Innovation in Education* by Sonny Magana. Thousand Oaks, CA: Corwin, www.corwin.com. Reproduction authorized only for the local school site or nonprofit organization that has purchased this book.

Transcendent Technology Use

A guide for evaluating teachers' integration of digital tools for the transformational technology use stage T3.1: Inquiry Design is shown in Table 6.13. Consider using this guide to support teachers as they increase their competence and proficiency in this stage of technology integration. Note the inclusion of indicators for both teacher and student use of digital tools to enhance inquiry design tasks.

A guide for evaluating teachers' integration of digital tools for the transformational technology use stage T3.2: Social Entrepreneurship is shown in Table 6.14. Consider using this guide to support teachers as they increase their competence and proficiency in this stage of technology integration. Note the inclusion of indicators for both teacher and student use of digital tools to enhance social entrepreneurship tasks.

USING THE T3 FRAMEWORK FOR PROFESSIONAL AND ORGANIZATIONAL DEVELOPMENT

Will teachers' use of the T3 Framework result in improved instructional practices and student growth gains? This in no small way depends on both the nature of professional development that teachers experience on the T3 Framework and the manner in which those learning experiences are supported. Compounding evidence strongly suggests that teacher professional development that is complemented by classroom coaching activities has a higher probability of yielding significant improvements in the quality of classroom instruction (Haystead & Magana, 2013; Joyce & Showers, 1988; Magana, 2016).

In their seminal study, Joyce and Showers (1988) report:

> In studies that have asked the transfer question (e.g., did participants use new skills in the classroom, did they use them appropriately, did they integrate new skills with existing repertoire, was there long-term retention of the products of training), several findings emerge. First, the gradual addition of training elements does not appear to impact transfer noticeably (*ES [effect size] of .00* for information or theory; theory plus demonstration; theory, demonstration and feedback) . . . however, a large and dramatic increase in transfer of training (*ES 1.68*) occurs when in-class coaching is added to an initial training experience comprised of theory explanation, demonstration and practice with feedback. (pp. 71–72)

The impact of an instructional coach on knowledge transfer is so powerful that classroom coaching should be considered a necessary complement to teacher professional development focused on implementing the T3 Framework. Classroom coaches can help ensure that teachers are able to transfer the skills,

TABLE 6.13 ■ T3.1: Inquiry Design—Teacher Observation Guide

T3.1: Inquiry Design

What do I do to have students use digital tools for inquiry design during learning tasks?

The teacher facilitates students' use of digital tools to enhance inquiry design during learning tasks.	**Notes**
Teacher Evidence	**Student Evidence**
☐ Teacher facilitates students' use of digital tools to investigate a real-life wicked problem that matters to them.	☐ Students use digital tools to investigate a real-life wicked problem that matters to them.
☐ Teacher facilitates students' use of digital tools to design an original line of inquiry focused on generating a robust solution to the wicked problem.	☐ Students use digital tools to design an original line of inquiry focused on generating a robust solution to the wicked problem.
☐ Teacher facilitates students' use of digital tools to communicate, defend, and iterate their unique knowledge contribution to solve the wicked problem.	☐ Students use digital tools to communicate, defend, and iterate their unique knowledge contribution to solve the wicked problem.

Proficiency Scale (Use evidence checkpoints to determine level of proficiency.)

1. Beginning	2. Developing	3. Mastering
Not yet nearing agile, adaptive use of digital tools to enhance teaching and learning tasks that demonstrates little or no impact monitoring and critical errors or oversights	Nearing agile, adaptive use of digital tools to enhance teaching and learning tasks that demonstrates some impact monitoring and some critical errors or oversights	Agile, adaptive use of digital tools to enhance teaching and learning tasks that demonstrates impact mindfulness and is free from critical errors or oversights

Available for download at **www.corwin.com/disruptiveclassroomtech**

Copyright © 2017 by Corwin. All rights reserved. Reprinted from *Disruptive Classroom Technologies: A Framework for Innovation in Education* by Sonny Magana. Thousand Oaks, CA: Corwin, www.corwin.com. Reproduction authorized only for the local school site or nonprofit organization that has purchased this book.

TABLE 6.14 ■ T3.2: Social Entrepreneurship—Teacher Observation Guide

T3.2: Social Entrepreneurship

What do I do to have students use digital tools for social entrepreneurship during learning tasks?

The teacher facilitates students' use of digital tools to enhance social entrepreneurship during learning tasks.	**Notes**

Teacher Evidence	**Student Evidence**
☐ Teacher facilitates students' use of digital tools to imagine, design, and create new tools or platforms as solutions to wicked problems that matter.	☐ Students use digital tools to imagine, design, and create new tools or platforms as solutions to wicked problems that matter.
☐ Teacher facilitates students' use of digital tools to beta test, iterate, and generate robust versions of their digital solutions to wicked problems that matter.	☐ Students use digital tools to beta test, iterate, and generate robust versions of their digital solutions to wicked problems that matter.
☐ Teacher facilitates students' use of digital tools to scale the implementation of their robust digital solutions to wicked problems that matter.	☐ Students use digital tools to scale the implementation of their robust digital solutions to wicked problems that matter.

Proficiency Scale (Use evidence checkpoints to determine level of proficiency.)

1. **Beginning**	2. **Developing**	3. **Mastering**
Not yet nearing agile, adaptive use of digital tools to enhance teaching and learning tasks that demonstrates little or no impact monitoring and critical errors or oversights	Nearing agile, adaptive use of digital tools to enhance teaching and learning tasks that demonstrates some impact monitoring and some critical errors or oversights	Agile, adaptive use of digital tools to enhance teaching and learning tasks that demonstrates impact mindfulness and is free from critical errors or oversights

Available for download at **www.corwin.com/disruptiveclassroomtech**

Copyright © 2017 by Corwin. All rights reserved. Reprinted from *Disruptive Classroom Technologies: A Framework for Innovation in Education* by Sonny Magana. Thousand Oaks, CA: Corwin, www.corwin.com. Reproduction authorized only for the local school site or nonprofit organization that has purchased this book.

knowledge, and competencies gained during professional development training sessions into their actual classroom instructional practices.

When planning for professional development for technology integration using the T3 Framework as a guide, consider the evidence for including classroom coaching in your plans. Doing so will both complement these offerings and enhance your well-intentioned efforts to improve teaching and learning through professional development.

SUMMARY

Making the T3 Framework actionable is a core objective of this entire work. Technology integration models that are overly subjective, are ambiguous, or fail to use nominal increments for measurement and evaluation are prone to misinterpretation, misapplication, and erroneous assessment. Such looseness leaves ample room for much imprecision in the application of digital tools to enhance instructional and learning tasks. The result of such slackness is a pronounced diminishment of the potential impact that digital tools might have on these important goals.

The T3 Framework is designed to tighten up the process of integrating technology into teaching and learning by providing a clearer, more precise, and actionable framework to guide teachers and leaders in self-assessing current uses of technology, setting professional growth goals, and achieving continuously higher levels of mastery. This chapter provides tools and guidance to support teachers and leaders in these processes. This chapter also provides a guide for leaders to collaborate with teachers on monitoring and tracking progress toward their professional growth goals. It is my sincere hope that teachers, students, leaders, and whole education systems will become emancipated from errors of judgment and choice that lead to low-value technology use by applying a richer and more precise language to discuss it.

REFERENCES

Preface

Schwartz, P. (2010). Inevitable strategies. In G. R. Hickman (Ed.), *Leading organizations* (2nd ed., pp. 6–13). Thousand Oaks, CA: Sage.

Chapter 1

Bransford, J., Brown, A. L., Cocking, R. R. (2000). *How people learn: Brain, mind, experience and school*. Washington, DC: National Academy Press.

Cheung, A., & Slavin, R. E. (2011, July). *The effectiveness of educational technology applications for enhancing mathematics achievement in K–12 classrooms: A meta-analysis*. Baltimore, MD: Johns Hopkins University, Center for Research and Reform in Education.

Christensen, C. M., Horn, M. B., & Johnson, C. W. (2008). *Disrupting class: How disruptive innovation will change the way the world learns*. New York: McGraw Hill.

Cuban, L., Kirkpatrick, H., & Peck, C. (2001). High access and low use of technologies in high school classrooms: Explaining an apparent paradox. *American Educational Research Journal, 38*(4), 813–834.

Dewey, J. (1938). *Experience and education*. New York: Kappa Delta Pi.

Hattie, J. (2009). *Visible learning: A synthesis of over 800 meta-analyses relating to achievement*. New York: Routledge.

Hattie, J. (2012). *Visible learning for teachers: Maximizing impact on learning*. New York: Routledge.

Haystead, M., & Magana, S. (2013). *Using technology to enhance the art and science of teaching framework: A descriptive case study*. Centennial, CO: Marzano Research.

Haystead, M., & Marzano, R. J. (2009). *Evaluation study on the effect of Promethean ActivClassroom on student achievement*. Centennial, CO: Marzano Research.

Haystead, M., & Marzano, R. J. (2010). *A second year evaluation study of Promethean ActivClassroom*. Centennial, CO: Marzano Research.

Lennon, J. W., & McCartney, J. P. (1970). Because [Recorded by the Beatles]. On *Abbey Road* [CD]. London: Apple.

Magana, S. (2016). *Enhancing the art and science of teaching with technology: A model for improving learning for all students*. Unpublished doctoral dissertation, Seattle University, Seattle, Washington.

Magana, S., & Marzano, R. J. (2014a). *Enhancing the art and science of teaching with technology*. Bloomington, IN: Solution Tree.

Magana, S., & Marzano, R. J. (2014b). *Enhancing the art and science of teaching with technology webinar*. Retrieved September 21, 2015 from http://www.marzanoresearch.com/resources/webinars/enhancing-art-science-teaching-with-technology-ewp064

Marzano, R. J. (2004). *Building background knowledge for academic achievement*. Alexandria, VA: ASCD.

Marzano, R. J. (2007). *The art and science of teaching: A comprehensive framework for effective instruction.* Alexandria, VA: Association for Supervision & Curriculum Development.

Marzano, R. J., Pickering, D. J., & Pollock, J. E. (2001). *Classroom instruction that works: Research-based strategies for increasing student achievement.* Alexandria, VA: ASCD.

Mayer, R. (2001). *Multimedia learning.* New York: Cambridge University Press.

McFarlane, A. (2015). *Authentic learning for the digital generation: Realising the potential of technology in the classroom.* New York: Routledge.

Morris, D. (1968). *The naked ape.* New York: McGraw Hill.

Prensky, M. (2001). Digital natives, digital immigrants Part 1. *On the Horizon, 9*(5), 1–6.

Vygotsky, L. (1978). *Mind in society.* Cambridge, MA: Harvard University Press.

Chapter 2

Fairhurst, G. T. (2011). *The power of framing: Creating the language of leadership.* San Francisco: Jossey-Bass.

Lewin, K. (1947). Frontiers in group dynamics. *Human Relations, 1*(2), 150–151.

Magana, S., & Marzano, R. J. (2014). *Enhancing the art and science of teaching with technology.* Bloomington, IN: Solution Tree.

Mishra, P., & Koehler, M. J. (1998). TPACK.org. Retrieved October 5, 2015, from www.tpack.org

Puentedura, R. R. (2009). *As we may teach: Educational technology, from theory into practice* [Podcast]. Retrieved January 28, 2017, from http://www.hippasus.com/rrpweblog/archives/000025.html

Puentedura, R. R. (2013). SAMR: A contextualized introduction. Retrieved October 5, 2015, from http://www.hippasus.com/rrpweblog

Rittel, H., & Webber, M. (1973). Dilemmas in a general theory of planning. *Policy Sciences, 4*, 155–169.

Van Halen, E. L. (1978). Eruption [Recorded by Van Halen]. On *Van Halen I* [CD]. Los Angeles, CA: Warner Brothers Records.

Wallace, D. F. (2005, May 21). *This is water.* Kenyon College commencement address. Retrieved December 18, 2016, from https://www.youtube.com/watch?v=IYGaXzJGVAQ

Chapter 3

Einstein, A. (N/A). Although this quote is generally attributed to Albert Einstein, there is some equivocation as to whether he actually ever said it. For an interesting read on this, see http://www.salon.com/2013/08/06/the_definition_of_insanity_is_the_most_overused_cliche_of_all_time/

Magana, S., & Marzano, R. J. (2014). *Enhancing the art and science of teaching with technology.* Bloomington, IN: Solution Tree.

Marzano, R. J. (2007). *The art and science of teaching: A comprehensive framework for effective instruction.* Alexandria, VA: ASCD.

Mayer, R. (2001). *Multimedia learning.* New York: Cambridge University Press.

National Education Association. (2008). *Access, adequacy, and equity in education technology: Results of a survey of America's teachers and support professionals on technology in public schools and classrooms.* Washington, DC: Author. Retrieved April 2, 2015, from http://www.edutopia.org/pdfs/NEA-Access, Adequacy,andEquityinEdTech.pdf

Chapter 4

Dreikurs, R. (1964). *Children the challenge*. New York: Penguin Books.

Dweck, C. (2006). *Mindset: The new psychology of success*. New York: Ballantine Books.

Freire, P. (1973). *The pedagogy of the oppressed*. New York: Seabury Press.

Hattie, J. (2009). *Visible learning: A synthesis of over 800 meta-analyses relating to achievement*. New York: Routledge.

Hattie, J. (2012). *Visible learning for teachers: Maximizing impact on learning*. New York: Routledge.

Haystead, M., & Magana, S. (2013). *Using technology to enhance the art and science of teaching framework: A descriptive case study*. Denver, CO: Marzano Research.

Haystead, M., & Marzano, R. J. (2009a). *Evaluation study on the effect of Promethean ActivClassroom on student achievement*. Centennial, CO: Marzano Research.

Haystead, M., & Marzano, R. J. (2009b). *Meta-analytic synthesis of studies conducted at Marzano Research on instructional strategies*. Centennial, CO: Marzano Research.

Haystead, M., & Marzano, R. J. (2010). *A second year evaluation study of Promethean ActivClassroom*. Centennial, CO: Marzano Research.

Magana, S. (2016). *Enhancing the art and science of teaching with technology: A model for improving learning for all students*. Unpublished doctoral dissertation, Seattle University, Seattle, Washington.

Magana, S., Lovejoy, J., Nafissian, D., & Reynaud, G. (1993). *The Washington schools change project: What happens when a modem is placed in classrooms*. Olympia, WA: OSPI.

Magana, S., & Marzano, R. J. (2014). *Enhancing the art and science of teaching with technology*. Bloomington, IN: Solution Tree.

Magana, S., & Marzano, R. J. (2015). Leveraging technology, increasing performance. In J. Bellanca (Ed.), *Connecting the dots: Teacher effectiveness and deeper professional learning* (pp. 181–202). Bloomington, IN: Solution Tree.

Marzano, R. J. (2007). *The art and science of teaching*. Alexandria, VA: ASCD.

Mazur, E. (2009, November 12). *Confessions of a converted lecturer: Eric Mazur* [Video]. Retrieved from https://www.youtube.com/watch?v=WwslBPj8GgI

Meyer, A., Rose, D. H., & Gordon, D. (2014). *Universal design for learning: Theory and practice*. Wakefield, MA: CAST Professional Publishing.

Ritchhart, R., Church, M., & Morrison, K. (2011). *Making thinking visible: How to promote engagement, understanding, and independence for all learners*. San Francisco: Jossey-Bass.

Roessger, K. M. (2016). Skills-based learning for reproducible expertise: Looking elsewhere for guidance. *Journal of Vocational Education & Training, 68*(1), 118–132.

Toffler, A. (1970). *Future shock*. New York: Random House.

Chapter 5

Barnes, M., & Gonzales, J. (2015). *Hacking education: 10 quick fixes for every school*. Cleveland, OH: Times 10 Publications.

Delaney, J. R. (2015, January 5). Interactive oceans. Retrieved from http://ooi.washington.edu/rsn/jrd/bio.html

Gray, D. E. (2014). *Doing research in the real world*. Thousand Oaks, CA: SAGE.

Lacy, S. (2012, May 15). The irony of the social media era: It was created by the world's least social people. *Huffington Post*. Retrieved May 1, 2016, from http://www.huffingtonpost.com/sarah-lacy/social-media-entrepreneurs-mark-zuckerberg_b_1518471.html

Magana, S. (1994). *The Polar Project: A collaborative action research project on integrating telecommunications technology at ACES High School*. Unpublished master's thesis, City University, Seattle, Washington.

Magana, S., Henly, J., Murphy, M., Rayl, G., & Travis, J. (1996). *The Illinois student project information network project report*. Springfield: Illinois State Board of Education.

Magana, S., & Marzano, R. J. (2014). *Enhancing the art and science of teaching with technology*. Bloomington, IN: Solution Tree.

Morrison, A. (2013). *Homegrown honeybees: An absolute beginner's guide*. North Adams, MA: Storey.

Resnick, M. (2014, November 11). Mitch Resnick—MIT Media Lab: Lifelong Kindergarten [Video]. *Lifelong Kindergarten*. Retrieved July 14, 2016, from https://llk.media.mit.edu/news/10

Resnick, M., & Siegel, D. (2015). A different approach to coding: How kids are making and remaking themselves from Scratch. *Bright: What's New in Education?* Retrieved February 14, 2016, from https://medium.com/bright/a-different-approach-to-coding-d679b06d83a#.5dcstj8hh

Rothbard, S. (2015, February 13). Eddie Van Halen Smithsonian talk [Video]. *Van Halen News Desk*. Retrieved March 20, 2016, from http://www.vhnd.com/2015/02/13/video-eddie-van-halens-smithsonian-speech

Schilling, D. R. (2013, April 19). Knowledge doubling every 12 months, soon to be every 12 hours. *Industry Tap*. Retrieved April 14, 2016, from http://www.industrytap.com/knowledge-doubling-every-12-months-soon-to-be-every-12-hours/3950

Shapiro, R. A. (Ed.). (2013). *The real problem-solvers: Social entrepreneurs in America*. Stanford, CA: Stanford University Press.

Snapp, M. (2016). How an 11-year-old CEO is using tech to help save honeybees. *Huffington Post*. Retrieved August 12, 2016, from http://www.huffingtonpost.com/mary-snapp/11-year-old-ceo-using-tech-to-save-bees_b_10719682.html

Thayer, H. (1993). *Polar dream: The first solo expedition by a woman and her dog to the magnetic North Pole*. Troutdale, OR: NewSage Press.

Wanshel, E. (2016). Teen makes 'Sit With Us' app that helps students find lunch buddies. *Huffington Post*. Retrieved September 16, 2016, from http://www.huffingtonpost.com/entry/teen-creates-app-sit-with-us-open-welcoming-tables-lunch-bullying_us_57c5802ee4b09cd22d926463

Chapter 6

DuFour, R., & Eaker, R. (1998). *Professional learning communities at work: Best practices for enhancing student achievement*. Bloomington, IN: National Education Service.

Fuchs, L. S., & Fuchs, D. (1986). Effects of systematic formative evaluation: A meta-analysis. *Exceptional Children, 53*, 199–208.

Gray, D. E. (2014). *Doing research in the real world*. Thousand Oaks, CA: SAGE.

Hattie, J. (2009). *Visible learning: A synthesis of over 800 meta-analyses relating to achievement*. New York: Routledge.

Haystead, M., & Magana, S. (2013). *Using technology to enhance the art and science of teaching framework: A descriptive case study*. Centennial, CO: Marzano Research.

Joyce, B., & Showers, B. (1988). *Student achievement through staff development*. New York: Longman.

Kahneman, D. (2011). *Thinking, fast and slow.* New York: MacMillan.

Magana, S. (2016). *Enhancing the art and science of teaching with technology: A model for improving learning for all students.* Unpublished doctoral dissertation, Seattle University, Seattle, Washington.

Magana, S., & Marzano, R. J. (2014). *Enhancing the art and science of teaching with technology.* Bloomington, IN: Solution Tree Press.

Marzano, R. J. (2007). *The art and science of teaching: A comprehensive framework for effective instruction.* Alexandria, VA: ASCD.

Marzano, R. J. (2012). *Becoming a reflective teacher.* Bloomington, IN: Solution Tree.

Schön, D. A. (1983). *The reflective practitioner: How professionals think in action.* New York: Basic Books.

INDEX

Applications. *See* T3 Framework applications
Ashoka, 84
Audacity tool, 50
Automation stage/T1.1, 28–29
    clarifying questions/value indicators for,
        29, 29 (table)
    continuous improvement and, 31
    education technology tools, task automation
        and, 20 (table), 29–31
    framing tool for, 32
    professional goal setting and, 95 (table)
    reflective practice and, 31
    See also Consumption stage/T1.2;
        Translational technology use/T1

Beckett, S., 3, 6
Brandford, J., 7
Brown, A. L., 7

Christensen, C. M., 4
Class-sourcing, 56–57
ClassFlow tool, 50
Cloud-based word processing, 50, 59
Cocking, R. R., 7
Code blocks, 77
Community orientation, xviii, 76
Constructivist learning theory, 8
Consumption stage/T1.2, 31
    clarifying questions/value indicators
        for, 33, 33 (table)
    consumption, definition of, 31
    digital divide, bridging of, 33, 35
    digital resources for, 35
    digitally accessible content and, 33
    framing tool for, 34
    multisensory digital media and, 33
    professional goal setting and, 96 (table)
    prosumer revolution and, 42
    See also Automation stage/T1.1; Translational
        technology use/T1
Continuity principle, 6
Contribution stage/T2.2, 53
    clarifying questions/value indicators
        for, 54, 54 (table)

class-sourcing and, 56–57
classroom promises/commitments
    development and tracking/T2.2–1 and,
    54–55, 55 (table)
digital artifacts, production/exhibition of, 53
digital tools for, 55 (table), 57–59, 59 (table)
framing tool for, 60
interdependent learning communities and,
    53–54, 58–59
portfolios/process-folios and, 59
professional goal setting and, 98 (table)
student-produced tutorial curation/T2.2–3
    and, 57–59, 59 (table)
student-produced tutorial production/T2.2–2
    and, 56–57
teacher evaluation process and, 105 (table)
See also Production stage/T2.1;
    Transformational technology use/T2

Dewey, J., 6, 7, 11
Digital divide, 33, 35
Digital natives, 11
Digital technologies. *See* T3 Framework
    applications; Technology
    integration principles
Disruptive innovation, 3, 19
    accessible/manageable change and, 4
    change, negative reaction to, 3, 4
    disruption, discomfort with, 3–4
    disruption, positive force of, 4
    disruptive innovation theory and, 4
    distractive innovation and, 5, 6
    education, disruptive transitions in, 5–6
    educational technologies, increased
        prevalence of, 15
    mastery orientation and, 3
    novelty effect and, 5
    student engagement/performance and, 5–6
    technological determinism and, 6
    traditional pedagogy and, 4
    21st century skills and, 3, 6
    See also Disruptive technologies; Effective
        pedagogy; T3 Framework
Disruptive innovation theory, 4

117

A SAGE Publishing Company

Helping educators make the greatest impact

CORWIN HAS ONE MISSION: to enhance education through intentional professional learning.

We build long-term relationships with our authors, educators, clients, and associations who partner with us to develop and continuously improve the best evidence-based practices that establish and support lifelong learning.

Solutions you want. Experts you trust. Results you need.

AUTHOR CONSULTING

Author Consulting

On-site professional learning with sustainable results! Let us help you design a professional learning plan to meet the unique needs of your school or district. www.corwin.com/pd

INSTITUTES

Institutes

Corwin Institutes provide collaborative learning experiences that equip your team with tools and action plans ready for immediate implementation. www.corwin.com/institutes

ECOURSES

eCourses

Practical, flexible online professional learning designed to let you go at your own pace. www.corwin.com/ecourses

READ2EARN

Read2Earn

Did you know you can earn graduate credit for reading this book? Find out how: www.corwin.com/read2earn

Contact an account manager at (800) 831-6640 or visit **www.corwin.com** for more information.

CORWIN